The Key to Healthy Prostate and Andropause

Information and Action

Sighi Drassinower

and

Frank Fabian

Published by:
Nature's Life & Health Inc.
1121 Crandon Blvd. Suite D 604, Key Biscayne, FL 33149

ISBN: 0-9665349-0-5

The purpose of this book is to educate. Neither the authors
nor the publisher will have the liability or responsibility for
any injury caused or alleged to be caused directly or indirectly
by the information contained in this book. This book is not
medical advice. To obtain appropriate recommendation to a
particular situation, please consult a qualified specialist.

Contents

This book is dedicated to all the patients suffering from prostate problems and to every man suffering from andropause. Especially for every man over 35 who doesn't have any symptoms now and have a unique opportunity to proactively do something about it. After reading this book you will have the information you need to act. I hope you will.

The Undertaking

After many years of research, there is real evidence that aging can be slowed, prolonging youth and maintaining health for a longer period of time. The purpose of this series of books is to inform the public as to what steps the anti-aging medical community recommends in order to prevent aging.

This is the first of a series of fiften books that deals with the subject of healthy aging.

The beginning of this book will deal with the subject of healthy aging in general.

Then specific topics are developed, including the topic of the healthy prostate.

Yes, this whole undertaking is very ambitious. The probability of making mistakes increases with the magnitude of the project, as Will Durant, the famous American historian (1885-1978), put it.

On the other hand, little has been done to systematically evaluate the great achievements in medicine in regards to aging. People need to be informed, and this knowledge certainly can be understood and applied by everyone.

After every chapter, the reader will find the key information repeated in a simple, understandable, and useable way. You will find that most of these can be taken into action immediately.

This book has been written for the general public, the medical layman. Great efforts have been made to define complicated terms easily so that their understanding is possible and attainable.

The effort is definitely worth it; because the goal of this book and those that follow in this series is that you can stay young and healthy for a long time.

Sighi Drassinower, MD, and Frank Fabian

Florida, November 2004

I

Good News, Good News, Good News

Since the anti-aging movement started in 1993, not a week has gone by without good news in relation to staying young. The anti-aging movement gained international recognition, and health care systems in several nations are providing new services. And yes, the biological age (as opposed to the chronological age) is diminishing every year. One can be seventy-five years old and feel fifty-five. Amazing! Longevity is not a dream anymore. It is an attainable. A vital life span of one hundred twenty years is within reach. Medical knowledge is doubling every three-and-a-half years. Huge advances have been made in cell research, in manipulating atoms and molecules, and in nearly all medical disciplines.

Influenza, diarrhea, and pneumonia, the main causes of death about a century ago, are not a threat anymore. Techniques to rebuild lost brain and nerve tissue are in progress. Bone regrowth is within reach. There are literally hundreds of techniques existing already for the strengthening of the immune system. Maybe pain, disability, and disease will one day be taught only in history class. Who knows?

We do know that proper diet stops or slows down aging and that unbelievably sophisticated nutritional supplements now exist. We know of hormone therapies, the importance of exercise, and the benefit of vitamins, minerals, and antioxidants. And the best is: we get wiser everyday. So the years of getting fat, having a belly, an expanding waist, losing hair, and a waning sex life are now optional. Unhealthy aging is optional. The three main diseases that cause death today can be prevented.

Heart disease causes death in 31.4 percent of Americans, cancer in 23.3 percent, stroke in 6 precent. These three major causes of death in America are under scientific assault. Today there are numerous techniques and treatments against the typical aging diseases such as Alzheimer's disease, non-insulin dependent diabetes, osteoporosis, autoimmune disorders, arthritis, and Parkinson's disease. They are, by far, not perfect, but we may be entering a golden age in the study of health, especially due to the pace at which medical research progresses today.

Additionally, there is some common knowledge today about aging: We know exercise is important. We know proper nutrition is a must. We know that eliminating alcohol, cigarettes, and drugs is helpful. We know a healthy environment is important. We know polluted air and water, pesticides in our food, hormone, antibiotics, fungicides, and many chemicals in our foods are detrimental to our health, and some know that even electromagnetic fields created by all the electric appliances we use daily should be avoided. We know that maintaining a regular sleep pattern, having optimal weight, drinking purified or bottled water, and taking regular nutritional supplements are essential.

We know all this because of anti-aging-research.

Anti-aging is the talk of the day.

Anti-aging medicine is the newest and fastest growing clinical medical specialty. It focuses on aggressive preventive health care and goes far beyond cholesterol testing and mammograms.

Anti-aging medicine encompasses life style, hormone replacement therapies, antioxidants, and vitamin supplements to reduce free radical damage.

Clinical testing protocols not only measure hormone levels, but analyze the critical metabolic factors that control life itself, right down to the cellular level.

Ronald Klatz, the president and founder of American Academy of Anti-Aging Medicine, states:"Aging in not inevitable. Biomedical technologies available to your doctor can detect, prevent, treat, and even reverse many age-related disorders. Life spans of one hundred to one hundred twenty will become reality for today's baby boomers."

Every 7.7 seconds a baby boomer turns fifty. We have seventy-seven million baby boomers in the United States, and there are approximately seven thousands centenarians in the United States. This number will increase to one hundred sixty thousand by the year 2010. Without a doubt, we are entering a new age of anti-aging medicine with new approaches.

Enhanced immune system, improvement of memory and cognitive functions, increase of sexual energy, improvement of skin tone and texture, increased muscle strength, increased energy levels, and improvement of muscle to fat ratio are already possible and can be achieved, and more will come.

But wait a minute. You might say: this may all be true, but what can we do to achive those results? We often do not know how to immediately apply what we learn. This is the reason why this information has been put together. It is difficult to know what information to glean from all the information we are bombarded with every day. Some products are merely illusions or quirks. We need an evaluation of this information that can lead us directly into action. The most evective tool against aging is an analytical evaluation of the information available.

If the data is not evaluated, one is usually overwhelmed with all sorts of "information trash," as it has been called.

Literally thousands of information sources have to be evaluated to find the common workable denominators for healthy aging. All of the literature and information about aging has to be examined.

That is exactly what the authors tried to do in the following pages. They evaluated all the volumes of information. But who are these authors? Allow us to toot our own horn a little bit, because we think it is only fair for you to know with whom you are dealing.

Dr Sighi Drassinower was born in Peru. He graduated as an MD in 1985 from the Peruvian university, Cayetano Heredia, a leading university in Latin America. His father was a world-renowned allergist and immunologist who came to Peru from his native Austria and practiced medicine for more than fifty years. Working with his father for many years, Dr. Drassinower was always interested in preventive medicine, research, and education. Despite being an MD, for the last ten years he committed himself to the research of natural medicine. After attending many conferences of the American Academy of Anti-Aging Medicine, ACAM (American College of Advancement in Medicine), functional medicine, ortho molecular medicine, and many other seminars and conferences related to natural supplements and natural medicine, he became absolutely convinced that proactive preventive medicine and anti-aging medicine is the right way to practice medicine today.

He is a member of the American Academy of Anti-Aging Medicine and a Board Certified Physician, American Board of Anti-Aging Medicine, under the auspices of Harvard University. The third generation of doctors in his family is on its way. His daughter, Daphnie, is graduating as an MD in two years. Dr. Drassinower checks what students study now in medical school, but he believes it is not much different than thirty years ago. The next generation of doctors is going to have the same approach as he did: try to solve symptoms with drugs and not proactively prevent the causes of their patients' health problems.

The second author, Frank Fabian is a best-selling author

who has written quite a few books and is a specialist in putting data together, so you can easily understand it and can apply it as soon as possible.

To make a long story short, the following information involves many years of research, requiring the evaluation of hundreds of books and articles, attending many conferences and symposiums, and treating many patients, including ourselves. The following information is as accurate and as factual as possible. At the same time, this information is kept simple so you can understand it easily, but not at the cost of hiding from the reader essential scientific information and knowledge.

In 1993, a group of physicians and scientists started a movement and coined the word anti-aging, declared a war against aging. Dr. Drassinower is part of that movement.

Now the American Academy of Anti-Aging Medicine has more than twelve thousand members all over the world. All these members agree that aging is a treatable medical condition.

We admit one cannot stop chronological time. Years will pass and will add to our personal calendar, but we can try to slow, stop, and even reverse the aging process. We can try to act preventively and look for health problems before they strike. We can use information and knowledge to look for health problems and do something about them. Finding problems at the beginning and not waiting until they threaten our lives is key. In order to succeed, we have to be thorough. To keep it simple: it is not wise to follow the conventional methods of medicine, which is oriented toward treating symptoms when they become obvious. Most often, waiting until symptoms become obvious is too late.

At the same time we should look at all the possible sources of information. We should listen to our bodies, learn from our family history, and detect minor signs, symptoms, and biomarkers that can lead us to prevent, intervene, and treat health problems early. You can compare it to an intelligence department that fights terrorism in the world. Information is very important to make the right decisions.

Unfortunately, the conventional doctor does not have the time or the in-depth knowledge to really inform you on how to prevent disease and the deterioration of your body. So you have to provide yourself with enough knowledge to help yourself. Helping yourself is usually the only approach.

Why? Medicine is not preventive yet. We have a symptom-oriented medicine. We try to fix our bodies when something is already broken. We have to act before, not after, the problem arises.

Your doctor has to see twenty, thirty, forty, and sometimes fifty patients a day, every day. Do you really think the doctor can go in-depth and study your case to find out early signs, symptoms, or biomarkers that can lead the doctor to diagnose and prevent early health problems? Impossible!

Besides, most of the time insurance companies and Medicare will not pay for preventive medicine tests and treatments. They only pay for "medically necessary" ones. This unfortunately means that only when the health problem already is established and is hurting you, will insurance companies pay for it. However, we need to act preemptively. For this, you need guidance, and you need to be updated.

Updated information will help you to act fast. And here's more good news. A variety of natural health supplements exist today that are nothing less than stunning. At the end of each chapter, you will find a list of supplements, supported by the latest scientific findings, which will enable you to *do* something without any side effects. These are the advantages of the following pages.

The following information summarizes all advantages of reading this book.

This book contains an evaluation of information of thousands of books and articles.

It has been compiled by an MD, who professionally deals with the subject of aging on a scientific basis and is Board Certified (American Board of Anti-Aging Medicine).

It is presented as simply as possible.

It contains the most recent scientific results.

It leads you to immediate action.

It enables you to act preventively, to dramatically change your life-style, reduce environmental aggression, eat healthy, and use high quality natural supplements that have been scientifically proven to be useable over a long period of time without side effects.

Ready for and adventure?

Keep on reading.

Action

Information: The anti-aging movement started in 1993. The biological age as opposed to the chronological age can diminish every year. Longevity is not a dream anymore. It is an attainable fact.

Action: Decide to get all the information available as soon as possible.

Information: Anti-aging medicine focuses on aggressive preventive health care. The problem is the evaluation of information. Literally thousands of books and articles have to be evaluated, as well as hundreds of conferences and symposiums.

Action: The following information does just that, it is an evaluation of the information that allows you to preemptively act before a health problem strikes.

Information: You need updated information, natural health supplement information, simple information, and action-oriented information.

Action: Keep on reading.

Information: Anti-aging know-how exists in relation to prostate problems, menopause, immune system, heart diseases, joint, bones, diet, cancer, stroke, diabetes, osteoporosis, arthritis, and even Alzheimer's. All those diseases are under scientific assault.

Action: You have to get this anti-aging information early enough to prevent diseases from striking.

II.

Nothing but Facts

Before we start giving you the "key to healthy aging," let us first consider the facts.! We all know that today we generally live longer, and that is indeed good news, in fact very good news. We know that the countries with the highest life expectancy are the United States, Denmark, Great Britain, Finland, Belgium, Greece, Germany, The Netherlands, Israel, Luxemburg, New Zealand, Norway, Singapore, Spain, Austria, France, Italy, Canada, Australia, Sweden, Switzerland, Monaco, San Marino, and Japan in that sequence. In the U.S., in the year 1796, shortly after the French Revolution, one lived an average of twenty-five years; in 1896, forty-eight years; and today, seventy-seven years.

In the United States, people can expect to live an average of seventy-seven years; in Great Britain, 77.5 years; in Greece and Germany, a little more than seventy-eight years; in Austria, seventy-nine years; in Australia and Sweden, eighty years; in Switzerland, a little more than eighty years; and in Japan, about 81.5 years.

These statistics from U.C Berkely, give us the first answer: do people in some countries live longer? When the income is higher, when the "civilization" is "advanced," and when stable work is available, people live longer. This is, by the way, the reason, why people in China die at age seventy and in Russia within sixty-five years. In India, the life expectancy is a little more than sixty, in South Africa it's fifty, in Afghanistan it's forty-five, and in Angola only thirty-five years of age.

We know these facts, and, just by knowing the statistics, we can learn that environment, civilization, working opportunities, safety, and a good life, are responsible for longer living. We also know without a doubt (more than two thousand five hundred statisticians in one hundred ten countries supply us with data) that our life expectancy is continuously rising. Every year we live, we can expect to live six to eight weeks longer than the generation before us. "Long living," in the "good countries," (United States, middle, south, and west Europe, Japan, Australia, etc.) guarantees more or less that we continuously live longer. The statisticians tell us that in some countries those born after the year 2000 can expect to live one hundred years on average. Not bad. Not bad at all.

But we know even more. We know that women on average live longer than men. The reason for that: is woman having, if at all, heart attacks an average ten years later than men. Men usually live a more risky life, have more stress, and experience the ups and downs of the job more intensely. Additionally, men on average have more addictions than women.

Finally, we know that somebody who is happily married usually lives a longer life. The reasons for that are obvious: we are social beings and we need company, somebody with whom to share our thoughts, feelings, illusions. We seek affection and security, and a committed relationship provides both. Communication, a stable partnership, and trust make life easier. Cheerfulness and happiness are often attributed to a good relationship. We know that.

We do know a lot, but when it comes to the analysis of why people live longer, some a lot longer, even the experts have different opinions. However, the following "Whys" have been established without a doubt:

1. If you are married and you have a good stable relationship, your chance to live longer is very high. Divorced individuals and ones without a partner live a more stressful life. Emotional well- being is the key.
2. Having a job that is not too stressful is very important

for healthy aging.

3. We also know that the money we make plays an important role. The better our financial situation, the longer we live on average. Economically, the "upper classes," that is to say people who earn more, have a better chance of living longer. Poverty is one reason why people die at a younger age. People with a really low-income die four to six years earlier than people in the higher income brackets. Also people with a regular income live longer than people with little or no income. Economic stability matters.

4. It is not only the money that counts. A good education and having a respectable profession and living standards (housing/environment) are, without a doubt, factors that influence the length of our lives

5. Good nutrition, regular sleep, and exercise are all part of a healthy life. We know that alcohol, drug abuse, and tobacco are factors that lead to a shorter life.

6. We also know that advanced medical care is responsible for increasing the average life span. Medical doctors are saving lives. Experts differ here in their opinions, but we can say that good medical care is responsible for adding an average of six years to the normal life span. Surgery, anesthesia, and antibiotics help with illnesses like cancer, heart, liver, and lung disease, etc., and therefore lead to a longer life.

On the other hand, it is only fair to say there are also major problems. Let us name three:

1. Do we generally have healthy aging medicine? The answer is a categorical no. The fact is that overmedication and taking the wrong medication can shorten your life. According to a tudy done by J. Lazarou and published in JAMA in 1998, evey year in the US, 106,000

patients die in hospitals because of their medication. The fourth cause of death is complications with medication. We have an epidemic of cancer, heart disease, obesity, arthritis, chronic fatigue, fibromyalgia, Parkinson's disease, and many other degenerative diseases that come with aging. Our older population spends many hours in doctors' offices or hospitals and spends a lot of money in prescription medication just to treat symptoms, with many side effects. If the drug is giving causing a side effect, your doctor will probably prescribe another drug or will give you a drug to reduce the side effect of the first drug. This isn't the solution. The solution to this is simple: just look out for healthy aging medicine. Do not listen to the drug advertisement, listen to those who tell you how to get old and stay healthy with life style changes, exercise, eating healthy, reduction of environmental aggression, pure water, and natural products. The only one who can change things is *you*. You can change the health system. You can arm yourself with information and knowledge and act. You can have a horizontal relationship with your doctor. Not a vertical, paternal relationship, but a democratic patient-physician relationship. The doctor should be your partner, your trainer, and your educator by teaching you how to prevent and early detect health problems and offer solutions.

2. Doctors are generally treated as "authorities," whose opinions one dare not challenge. At the same time, those "authorities" may have different opinions, often contradictory. What is the solution? Well, the only person who can change things is again *you*.

3. Additionally, what we don't know is the real problem:

The fact is that most of the people of tomorrow will chronologically grow older, but people often cannot pay the expenses of the future anymore. That is to say, our health insurance systems will collapse sooner or later. Why? No one can pay all those expenses in the long run. Medical care of tomorrow will be so expensive that many people won't be able to afford it anymore. This is already starting to happen.

But think again. More and more people get older and older today. The health expenses rise. The health system is more and more overburdened. One does not need to be a prophet to see a catastrophe at the end of the tunnel. Since we are getting older and older, experts predict that soon insurance rates (say in 2010) will dramatically increase, but who should pay the bills?

What does that mean for *you*?

It simply means that *you* have to take care of *yourself*! In fact, the only chance for many people is to take precautions. Only by taking precautions will many people get the chance to live longer. The health system itself will soon reach its borderline. It means that only know-how and knowledge will help the average person live a long life of good health. It means that those factors that help you live longer have to be better understood. It means that only specific sophisticated know-how can prevent you from suffering. It means that *you* have to take your destiny back into your own hands.

Let us look on this vicious cycle more clearly.

These are the facts:

Health insurance companies operate today with figures in relation to the average life span, which are often incorrect and outdated. As stated earlier, people live longer. That means health insurance companies will pay less, or they will raise the premiums so high that only a few can afford it. Like it or not, sooner or later we will face a collapse of the health insurance system. The politicians will help and can help, for a while, but only for a short time. Then they will see that even their pockets are empty. Health care and its associated costs have been the "talk of the day" for several years now. Political parties will fight for their voters, and we will see more and more debates on television about health care. In fact, this is already the case to some extent, but it will increase. It will get worse.

Both parties, the Democrats and the Republicans, will sooner or later admit that health care systems cannot be endlessly supported. When the "social expenses" get too high, they damage the general economy. When the general economy is slowed down, the result is that the state has even less money in its pockets, and can pay less. So the state will sooner or later give the responsibility back to its citizens. And that means that the only one who can do something about it is *you*.

It is exactly for that reason that this book has been written. It has been written with the purpose to providing you with knowledge. The fact is if you know enough about aging, your chances of staying healthy are very good. There is an enormous amount of knowledge in relation to healthy aging. It is a subject in itself. It is a subject that is not difficult to grasp. It is a discipline that can be mastered, and that has to be mastered, if you want to live a long and healthy life. It is a subject that is even exciting and suspenseful. What is more interesting than finding out new things about life?

At the same time, you must know that science is a neverending story. Nearly every day new inventions are made. The fact is that our knowledge today about healthy aging is by far greater than it has ever been. The following provides you with the data necessary for living a long and healthy life. The style we used is intentionally simple—not academic, not artificially complicated—because we want you to understand it.

It is a book you can *use*. It is a book you can apply to your daily life. It is a health adventure, an action-book.

This is exactly the way that the body and health should be looked at: as though it were a game with specific rules. The better you know the rules of the game, the better your chances to win. Let's play the game!

Action

Information: The countries with the highest life expectancy are: The United States (on average 77 years), Denmark, Great Britain, Finland, Greece, Belgium, Germany, The Netherlands, Israel, Luxemburg, New Zealand, Norway, Singapore, Spain, Austria, France, Italy, Canada, Australia, Sweden, Switzerland, Monaco, San Marino, and Japan (on average 80.5 years).
Action: Avoid living in countries with violence, low income, war, and political instability.

Information: People who are married live longer.
Action: Go for a long-lasting relationship.

Information: People with jobs live longer.
Action: Find a regular job that gives you satisfaction and a sense of purpose, but that does not entail stressing you out, even when you are older. If your job is too stressful, start practicing anti-stress measures: yoga, meditation, and exercise.

Information: People in the upper quarter of income live on average four to six years longer. These people spend money on themselves and invest in their health.
Action: Get your finances in order if you haven't done so already. Prioritize expenses so that you can spend money on what is really important to you.

Information: People with a good education live longer. Educate yourself so that you can lead a better life
Action: Never stop to live a strictly professional life, having fun, take care of yourself no matter how old you are. (Be active, be curious, and learn something new every day).

Information: Exercise, regular sleep, and good nutrition are paramount for a longer life.

Action: Decide to learn more about these subjects and work out a systematic program that works for you.

Information: We do not have a healthy aging medicine. Every year in the United States 106,000 patients die in hospitals because of their medications.

Action: In general, avoid drugs with side effects. Look for natural products.

Information: Doctors are too often considered unquestionable authorities.

Action: Look for doctors who have a democratic relationship with their patients. Think for yourself.

Information: The health insurance system will collapse sooner or later. Most people will not be able to pay the insurance costs anymore. Only know-how and knowledge will guarantee that you live a longer life in good health.

Action: Decide to learn more about the laws of the body, especially the aging body. Read this book.

III

The Immortal Man, Hormones, and Andropause

An old dream exists that man is immortal and will never die. We find this dream in many religions and philosophies in which there usually is a separation between the body and the soul. Religion promises immortality, but only of one's soul. Man has never stopped dreaming that he also could make the body live forever.

Science-fiction authors envision that one day a medicine will exist, or should we say,: a body- technology, which enables you to literally change everything the body consists of: arms and legs every organ, the head, and even the nervous system. In the end, you would have an "organic robot body" and could live forever. This dream may or may not become true. What is true today is the fact that it is possible to live with today's "body- technology" to one hundred years old–an amazing step forward.

But how is this progress possible? We know why men (in the next book we will look at women) age. Another discovery that can completely change the aging process and cancer is the Telomerase Theory of Aging. It is a new theory of aging that holds many promising possibilities. This theory was born from the surge of technological breakthroughs in genetics and genetic engineering. *Telomeres* are sequences of nucleic acids extending from the end of the *chromosomes*. In short, telomeres act to maintain the integrity of our chromosomes. Every time our cells divide, the telomere is shortened, leading to cellular damage and cellular death associated with aging. Scientists discovered that the key element in rebuilding our disappearing telomeres is the "immortalizing" enzyme telomerase-an enzyme found only in germ cells and cancer cells. Telomerase appears to repair and replace telomeres, manipulating the "clocking" mechanism that controls the life span of dividing cells. Future development of a telomerase inhibitor may be able to ease cancer cells from dividing and presumably convert them back into normal cells.

But what are *enzymes*? Enzymes are any of several complex proteins that are produced by cells and act in specific biochemical reactions. Enzymes are proteins that speed up a chemical reaction. Enzymes do their work without being changed or used up in the process. Now the enzyme telomerase can repair telomeres. The idea is that we can make our cells regenerate the telomere and become "immortal." And we can make cancer cells return to normal cells, by reducing the telomere at an accelerated speed, so the cancer cells will die in three months or so. Possibly this therapy can one day end cancer and will make humans live many more years.

I want to mention just one study that I find very interesting:

Accelerated telomere shortening in response to life stress. We all know that stress is very bad for your health.

Numerous studies demonstrate links between chronic stress and indices of poor health, including risk factors for cardiovascular disease and poorer immune function. Nevertheless, the exact mechanisms of how stress gets "under the skin" remain elusive.

The journal, *Proceedings of the National Academy of Science USA*, published an article in December 2004 by Elissa S. Epel, and others from the Department of Psychiatry,

University of California.

They investigated the hypothesis that stress impacts health by modulating the rate of cellular aging. Here they provide evidence that psychological stress—both perceived stress and chronicity of stress—are significantly associated with higher oxidative stress, lower telomerase activity, and shorter telomere length, which are known determinants of cell senescence and longevity.

To make it simple, stress will contribute to aging faster.

Hormones

But telomerase treatment is off in the future. Nevertheless, you should keep an eye on the latest scientific findings. What is at our fingertips today is hormone treatment. So many things have changed as to the treatment with hormones. With hormonal treatment; it is no exaggeration to say that we entered a new age in medicine. Let us first consider the basics.

We all know that men past age forty or fifty undergo enormous hormonal changes, and hormones play a key role in aging. But what are hormones for? The word stems from the Greek word *horman* (to excite), which in turn comes from the Greek word *horme* meaning *impulse.* Hormones give impulses. To be more exact, a hormone is a substance formed in an organ of the body (gland); this substance is then carried to another organ (or tissue), where it fulfills a specific purpose.

Hormones act in a hormone receptor site, a specific site in the cell. Like a key to its lock, they fit perfectly. Hormones are chemical messengers secreted into the bloodstream or extra cellular fluid. So what one cell secretes affects the functioning of other cells. Most hormones circulate in blood, coming into contact with essentially all cells. However, a given hormone usually affects only a limited number of cells, which are called *target cells.* A *target cell* responds to a hormone because it bears receptors for the hormone. In other words, a particular cell is a target cell for a hormone if it contains functional receptors for that hormone. Cells that do not have such a receptor cannot be influenced directly by that hormone.

Reception of a radio broadcast provides a good analogy. Everyone within range of a transmitter for National Public Radio is exposed to that signal. However, in order to be a National Public Radio target, and thus influenced directly by their broadcasts, you have to have a receiver tuned to that frequency.

Hormone receptors are found either exposed on the surface of the cell or within the cell, depending on the type of hormone. The binding of a hormone to its receptor triggers a cascade of reactions within the cell that affects its function.

Growth, sexual activity, and many other body functions are controlled or triggered by hormones. We have many hormones, which should be balanced, but when we age, these hormones usually become imbalanced.

The results are less than beneficial: the sex-drive lessens, fat tissue increases, and muscle mass decreases. Depression and fatigue sometimes follow. In the worst cases, heart disease, erectile dysfunction, or prostate disease begin—so something must change. It is a result of hormonal imbalance.

But which hormones are affected? Let us take a look at only *four* hormones for the moment: estrogen, testosterone, progesterone, and DHT (Dihydrotestosterone). We need to understand these four types of hormones to understand what is happening as we age.

Estrogen, a composed word from *estrus,* literally means, "periodic sexual excitement or heat," and points at any female sex hormones.

Testosterone is also a coined, synthetic, and invented word. *Testis* (same as testicle), *stero* (pointing to a certain group of chemical compounds), and *one* are in this word. Test-o-ster-ones pointing to the male sex hormone produced by the testicles. Men *and* women have both male and female hormones. By the way, do not be impressed by big words. They are usually very simple once they are taken apart.

But just for kicks, let us look a little bit deeper into those two types of hormones.

Estrogen is not one hormone; it is the name of a group of hormones. There are three main forms of estrogen found in the human body: *estrone, estradiol,* and *estriol,* also known as E1, E2, and E3 respectively. Estradiol (E2) is the primary estrogen produced by the ovaries. Estrone (E1) is produced in large amounts during pregnancy and is a breakdown product of estradiol. Estriol (E3) is also a weak estrogen and may have anti-cancer effects. Before menopause, estradiol is the predominant estrogen. After menopause, estradiol levels drop more than estrone so that now estrone is the predominant estrogen. A man over fifty usually has more estrogen than a fifty-year-old menopausal woman. There is also a group of compounds called *phytoestrogens (phyto = plant)* generally found in food, which can also have "estrogen-like" effects in the body.

Testosterone is responsible for normal growth and development of male sex organs and maintenance of secondary sex characteristics. It is the primary androgenic (*Andro* = Greek = *man*) hormone, and its production and secretion are the end product of a series of hormonal interactions. Testosterone is the most important representative of the male sex hormones collectively called *androgens.* During puberty, testosterone levels are at their lifetime peak. They begin to decline around age twenty-three. Testosterone itself is responsible for three major functions:

1. The development of secondary male sex characteristics. This also is called the androgenic functions of testosterone. Some examples of these characteristics are increased

growth of body hair, beard growth, deep voice, increased production of sebaceous glands, development of the penis, aggressiveness, sexual behavior, libido, and the maturation of sperm.

2. The acceleration of muscle build-up, the increase of the formation of red blood cells, and the increase in the process of regeneration, and the recovery time after injuries or illness. It is also responsible for stimulating the entire metabolism, which results in the burning of body fat.

3. The inhibition of a cycle, which regulates the amount of testosterone produced in the organism. In other words, if you have too much testosterone, your body will tell itself to reduce or even stop the production of it until the hormone is back down to its normal levels.

Now *DHT* (or Dihydrotestosterone) is another male hormone, the one, in fact, that is suggested to be the main cause for the shrinking of the hair follicles, which leads to hair loss, can cause prostate enlargement, and and also prostate cancer. DHT is formed when the male hormone testosterone interacts with a special enzyme: 5 apha reductase.

In relation to the term *progesterone,* let us stay simple. The term was invented in the year 1930. Progesterone stimulates the uterus to prepare it for pregnancy. In men, progesterone inhibits the harmful effects of excess estrogen on the male body.

We could even make it easier by stating that four hormones (No. 1, 2, 3, and 4) are important. They have special functions and complicated names. Those complicated names are (let us repeat):

ESTROGEN (estrone, estradiol, estriol)
TESTOSTERONE
DHT
PROGESTERONE

Names, just names! But we need those names to describe the optimal health condition. And now it gets really exciting.

Staying Balanced

Let's go back to our original thought. Those four hormones have to be in special balance to be optimal. Again, as we age, less testosterone is produced. A lot of physical manifestations follow: loss of hair, a bigger belly, weakening muscles, and lessened sex drive.

So what do we need to do?

We're letting you in on a secret: chemistry is *very* simple in the end. You need the right elements or compounds in the right quantity and quality. That is chemistry: quantity and quality. So what *is* the right quantity and quality?

You need to balance these four hormones: testosterone, progesterone, estradiol, and DHT. A good ratio between testosterone/progesterone/estradiol/DHT is 60/200/1/1.

It cannot be stated more simply.

There is a very simple way to explain the relation between testosterone, estrogen (estradiol), and DHT. Imagine a river. The main river is testosterone, and it will divide into three different small rivers: the first will be estradiol, the second river will be DHT, and the third will be free testosterone. When we are young, the main river (testosterone) has a lot of water...and most of that water will go to the free testosterone "river."

As we age, the production of the testosterone main river diminishes. Testosterone starts converting into estradiol and DHT and less into free testosterone. The imbalance starts, and prostate problems start. So all you have to do is maintain the right balance. When we are balanced, we are all set. So we have a golden formula here. The formula again is 60/200/1/1 of testosterone/progesterone/estradiol/DHT.

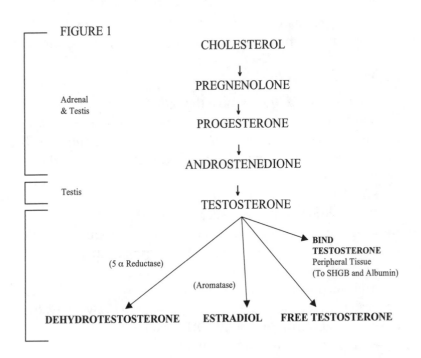

Figure 1: Pathway of testosterone formation in the testis and the conversion to DihydroTestosterone (DHT) and estradiol, in the peripheral tissues.

Testosterone in plasma is largely bound to proteins, mainly albumin (54 percent), SHBG (44 percent), and 2 percent is free testosterone. Nearly all albumin-bound testosterone is available for tissue uptake, so the bioavailability for testosterone in men is about 46 percent (equal to the free testosterone 2 percent plus albumin-bound fraction 44 percent). Adapted from **Williams Text-book of Endocrinology.** 10th Edition. Sanders 2003: P713-713.

Search for the Secret of Staying Young

Today we have this golden formula. But in the beginning of anti-aging research, not everything was so simple. In the beginning, scientists thought that testosterone alone would do the job. When scientists realized the importance of testosterone, they had a ball. They were thinking, all we have to do is: feed man with more testosterone, and he will stay young forever. Hormones (especially testosterone) were the talk of the day. Scientists were dancing on the tops of tables with joy. They thought they had invented man anew. Thousands and thousands experiments took place, but a lot were led in the wrong direction.

In the beginning, the following conclusions were drawn: Let us just produce artificial testosterone and all is fine. However, scientists found out that simple replacement therapy does not work. The reason: being is that testosterone converts (*aromatize* is the scientific word) into even *more* estrogen, worsening the condition. That is to say one gets older faster. Excess estrogen means increased risk of heart attacks, stroke, BPH (Benign Prostate Hypertrophy), the prostate growing bigger, too big, and prostate cancer. In other words, people were getting sicker. Testosterone injections, creams, and patches failed. Again,: testosterone could be converted to estrogen.

Much more extensive research was done, and a race began. It was discovered that testosterone is more than just a sex hormone. We use testosterone in the brain and in the heart; it improves oxygen uptake, controls blood sugar, is important for the immune system, the red blood cells, and a lot more. So obviously testosterone was the key. But bad news was suddenly the talk of the day: testosterone can produce prostate cancer. The medical world was shocked. Test after test, more research was done, costing millions of dollars. Up to today, there are at least twenty-seven scientific studies published. The results? There are twenty-two studies indicating that testosterone does *not* cause prostate cancer. However, there are also five studies indicating that testosterone *does* cause prostate cancer.

So what does one believe? This is what we know today: what produces prostate cell growth (which can cause cancer) is estrogen and DHT (Dihydrotestosterone) produced from testosterone. So you need to *reduce* these two hormones-and *not* the production of testosterone. So you do not need to castrate yourself with a scalpel or through chemical castration. The score is twenty-two to five against the theory that testosterone causes prostate cancer. Objectively, we conclude that the fear was over-emphasized.

However, more research was done, and it was exciting. Scientists found out again and again, how important testosterone is. It helped the coronary arteries. Low testosterone promoted cardiovascular diseases, raised blood pressure, and weakened the heart muscles. Fat increased with low testosterone. Some doctors became really excited, because it seemed to indicate that with testosterone, one could avoid taking all those horrible drugs usually prescribed to handle conditions like heart problems, fat, blood pressure, and other serious medical problems. Could all these problems come from low testosterone? Could an individual go into old age *without* all those drugs, which could have terrible side effects?

The vicious cycle usually was: take a drug against something, have side-effects, take a drug against those side-effects, have another side-effect, take drugs against those new side-effects. Thus, an endless cycle followed that was very dangerous for your health. But again, could depression and one hundred other illnesses be treated without dangerous drugs? Just by taking a good hormone or handling the hormonal imbalance could we be all set? Could that be true?

Scientists rolled up their sleeves. We were fighting depression with one drug for example. At the same time the libido—

the sex drive—got suppressed. We tried to handle inability to concentrate, moodiness, touchiness, irritability, timidity, inner unrest, and memory failure with drugs, and we felt heavily disappointed when we found out the vast number of side effects. We tried to handle passive attitudes, tiredness, even hypochondria with drugs—and forgot to test the hormone-balance-levels, (which can cause all that.) More and more enemies of the prescription drugs came up. The public, or part of the public, wanted to get away from those drugs. Horror stories came to light, and there were warnings about many drugs. Drugs, it seemed, had to be avoided by all means. People, in general, know that they dance with the devil when they are taking drugs.

So why not look for another alternative?

The show went on. More research was done. The hormone specialists pointed out again and again, what was related to testosterone deficiencies. Brain cell injury, arterial wall damage, and immune dysfunctions, all these symptoms had to do only with low testosterone. On the other hand, just giving an abundance of testosterone did not solve the problem. So some clever scientists tried a new approach: the suppression of estrogen. They tried both giving testosterone *and* suppressing estrogen at the same time. So much was sure: testosterone built protein, and the muscles improved cellular biogenetics, increased the metabolism, protected the heart, strengthened the heart muscles, and even helped to eliminate arrhythmia and angina, prevented blood clots, and prevented colon cancer. It was too good to be totally ignored.

Research went on. The factors that caused the estrogen and testosterone imbalance were more intensely researched. And one day, some scientist struck pure gold on a research line. It was found that one could *change* that imbalance.

Again, the golden formula of balance is 60/200/1/1 of testosterone/progesterone/estradiol/DHT.

With this formula, we can forget the earlier search and research. These are the latest findings, and, with this formula we unraveled, one of the major secrets of the human body.

Now let us look at this hormone problem from another angle, another perspective. The *male andropause* is intensely discussed today. What do we know for sure about this? And how can we apply the knowledge we already established safely?

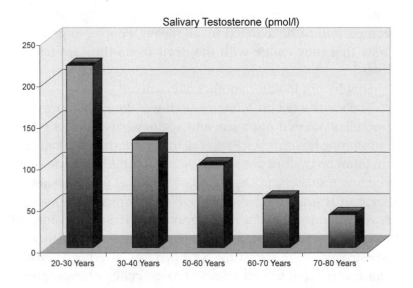

Chart 1: Salivary Testosterone.
We can see here how testosterone
levels decline with age.

Andropause, the Facts

First of all, what is it all about this mysterious *andropause?* What does it mean? Well, andropause is male menopause. As men age, testosterone levels go down, and conversion from testosterone to estrogen (estradiol) goes up. This is the definition in relation to hormones. By the time men are between the ages of forty and fifty-five, they can experience a phenomenon similar to the female menopause called andropause. Unlike women, men do not have a clear-cut signpost, such as the cessation of menstruation, to mark this transition. A drop in hormone levels, however, distinguishes both, estrogen in the female, testosterone in the male. The bodily changes occur very gradually in men and may be accompanied by changes in attitude and mood, fatigue, a loss of energy, sex drive, and physical agility. We hate it, but those are the facts.

What we may hate even more is that studies show this decline in testosterone can actually put an individual at risk for other health problems, such as heart disease and weak bones. Since all this happens at a time of life when many men begin to question their values, accomplishments, and direction in life, it is often difficult to realize that the changes occurring are not only related to external conditions. Unlike menopause, which generally occurs in women during their mid-forties to mid-fifties, a man's "transition" may be much more gradual and can expand over many decades. Attitude, stress, alcohol, injury, surgery, medication, obesity, and infection can contribute to its onset. Although with age, a decline in testosterone levels will occur in virtually all men, there is no way of predicting who will experience andropausal symptoms of sufficient severity to seek medical help. Nor can it be predicted at what age these symptoms will occur in any particular individual. Each man's symptoms may be different. You may ask: Is this a new phenomenon? Yes and no. In fact, andropause was first described in medical literature in the 1940s, so it is not really new. But our ability to *diagnose* it properly is. Sensitive tests for bioavailable testosterone were not available until recently, so andropause has gone through a long period where it was under- diagnosed and under-treated. Now that men are living longer, there is heightened interest in andropause, and this will help to advance our approach to this important life stage, which was identified so long ago. Another reason why andropause had been under-diagnosed over the years is that its symptoms can be vague and vary among individuals. Some men find it difficult to even admit that there is a problem. And many times physicians didn't think of low testosterone levels as a possible culprit. So these factors often led doctors to conclude that symptoms were related to other medical conditions (i.e., depression) or to aging and often encouraged their patients to accept that "they were no longer spring chickens." This situation is changing. New blood testing methods and saliva tests are available, and there is an increased interest in men's aging among medical researchers.

The idea that menopause is an experience exclusive to women is simply wrong. As husbands watch their wives, mothers, and sisters go through the hot flashes, night sweats, and mood swings of menopause, men may heave a sigh of relief that they don't have to go through it themselves. But in the face of physiology, we know that men are not, in fact, immune to the hormonal fluctuations of middle age. The effect may be more gradual, unlike the roller coaster many menopausal women find themselves on, but male menopause is a very real phenomenon. Again the name: Andropause. That's the textbook term for the midlife "pause" or decline in male hormone production of the androgens, specifically testosterone and DHEA. *DHEA?* Dehydroepiandrosterone is a hormone produced by the adrenal gland, and is a new hormone one needs to know about.

During the same time frame, estrogen, particularly estradiol, levels in males tend to increase as androgen levels decline. The result is a negative ratio between the two, a hormonal imbalance that typifies the andropause profile and signals an associated risk of prostate disease.

Functions of the Male Hormones

Let us repeat: The androgens increase energy and decrease fatigue. They help in maintaining erectile function and normal sex drive, and, in the anabolic (building) capacity, they are instrumental in increasing the strength of all structural tissues, including the skin, bones, muscles, and heart. Men make more testosterone than women, accounting for their generally greater muscle and bone mass. A proper balance of the androgenic hormones also helps to prevent depression and mental fatigue. These are the hormones that help provide the virility, stamina, and drive we associate with the make of the species. To make a long story short, they put the M in "macho."

Symptoms of Andropause

Needless to say, testosterone and DHEA levels in short supply are going to have a big impact on all those attributes both physical and mental that make men male. If at the same time levels of the female hormone estrogen are too high, which is not uncommon during this time, urinary and prostate problems may begin to enter the picture. Usually what the andropausal male notices first is a subtle loss of sexual desire, along with a downward shift in strength and energy. Bouts of depression and anxiety, the feeling of being "tired but wired," and a persistent lack of stamina are also common symptoms as the androgens downsize with age. The mid-life male quite often finds himself short on enthusiasm for the things he used to enjoy; work is not quite as challenging, and exercise is tougher. Fatigue sets in more quickly, and the only bedroom activity he's really up for is sleeping through the night, a feat too often sabotaged by frequent visits to the bathroom. Thinning hair, shrinking muscles, wrinkles, and an emerging pouch seem to go with the territory. He may feel rundown, anxious, edgy, and achy. If his stress quotient is too high, the male baby boomer may describe himself as "burned out," an indication that his cortisol levels are elevated. Now he is aging rapidly. One thing's for sure: he is not feeling like his old self.

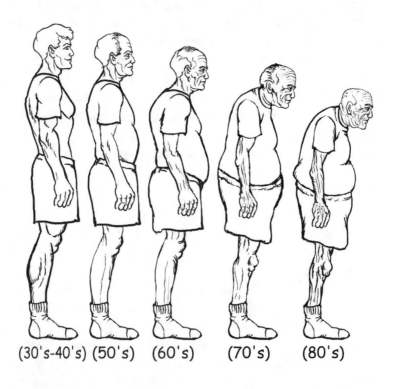

(30's-40's) (50's) (60's) (70's) (80's)

Aging Man: We can see in this illustration how a man can age. The lack of hormones, especially testosterone, will be reflected here by the loss of muscle mass, increase of fat tissue in the abdominal area, fatigue, depression, and wrinckles. The idea is to stay as much as possible as the man in his 30s.

Hormone Testing and Treatment

The first step toward restoring balance is to test hormone levels so as to identify specific deficiencies and excesses and to what extent they are out of range. This can be done through saliva testing in which optimal collection can take place in the privacy of one's own home and sent by regular mail for processing in the laboratory. Test results include a complete evaluation of hormone lab levels correlated with symptoms and hormone usage. The report serves as a rationale for patient and provider to determine the most suitable treatment for restoration of hormone balance and relief of symptoms. Stress management, exercise, proper nutrition, dietary supplements, and androgen replacement with physician guidance have all been shown to raise androgen levels in men and help to counter andropause symptoms.

Case studies from our files provide a snapshot of andropause:

A seventy-seven-year-old man complained of excessive fatigue, lack of stamina, loss of interest in sex, despite his recent marriage to an attractive younger woman, and general mental lethargy. His saliva testosterone level was found to be extremely low, and his estradiol (estrogen) levels were high, a profile commonly seen in late andropause. This man's cortisol tested low throughout the day. After consultation with his health care provider, he began supplementation with a bioidentical precursor of testosterone called androstenedione. *Androstenedione* is a hormone secreted by the adrenal gland, testicles, and ovaries. In normal men, less than 5percent of their testosterone comes from the conversion of adrenal androstenedione. The health care provider added progesterone to balance his excess estradiol (estrogen) level. This man rubbed a physiologic dose (tailored to his individual needs) of this natural hormone cream into his skin every morning and included in his regime adrenal supports, such as optimal nutrition, vitamins, morning walks, and an earlier bedtime.

Follow-up testing showed balanced levels of estradiol, progesterone, and testosterone along with great improvement in symptoms. According to this man, the testing and restoration of hormone balance gave him back his zest for life.

Another example: A fifty-three-year-old workaholic complained of loss of concentration, poor recovery from workouts, loss of muscle tone, and flagging energy. His capacity for exercise was much reduced, and his quality of sleep suffered from recurring urinary urgency throughout the night. This man tested his testosterone and his SHBG. Wait a minute. *SHBG?* Is it another sex hormone? SHBG is thought to be synthesized in the liver and in the circulation, and its biological function is the *transport* of certain sex hormones. Serum SHBG levels are relatively low at birth, increase to high levels during infancy, and then decrease during puberty. The highest physiologic levels of SHBG are observed in pregnant, near-term maternal serum. Just take SHBG (Sex Hormone Binding Globulin) as another name. This man also tested his PSA (prostate-specific antigen). PSA is a test used to screen for cancer of the prostate and to monitor treatment. PSA is a protein produced by the prostate gland. Although most PSA is carried out of the body in semen, a very small amount escapes into the blood stream.

He also completed a battery of other tests.

All levels were found to be out of range and out of balance in relation to one another. Stress management and supplementation with natural hormones was initiated. A topical gel to raise androgen levels, compounded with an aromatase inhibitor and progesterone to help lower estrogen levels, resulted in a balanced ratio of testosterone to estrogen. Our workaholic lost weight, had increased energy, improved his muscle tone, and reported an overall heightened sense of well-being. His family and marital life thrived under the new regime.

Again: News

So there is, in fact, a lot of good news in relation to andropause. And you've learned about two new hormones, in addition to the basic four hormones.

The point is, you can do something about andropause and the hormonal imbalance, and you don't have to take drugs.

However, you may wonder if there is some general advice when it comes to andropause.

What can you do to control andropause?

Well, there are six factors involved that cause hormonal imbalance.

Six Factors

So let us look at these six factors that can restore hormonal balance. Some of these factors may be utterly surprising; some are known.

Factor One: Lifestyle

Let us start with the simplest factor: lifestyle change.

It was discovered that alcohol, for example, produced a dramatic worsening in the hormonal balance. We obviouly don't want to put down the literally one hundred different alcoholic beverages—from wine to beer to liquors and all the brand names of whiskeys— but, without a doubt, alcohol is a major cause for declining health, for early aging, and for the imbalance of those hormones. So without alcohol, one doesn't age so fast.

Eating healthy, exercise frequently and reduction of stress are also very important factors.

Factor Two: Zinc Deficiency

It was discovered that zinc inhibits excess estrogen. But what is zinc? Zinc is a bluish -white, metallic chemical element (as we all know,) but it is helpful in many ways in the human body. Zinc is an essential mineral. More than one hundred zinc metalloenzymes have been identified in the human body. Zinc is important for protein metabolism, producing energy, maintaining healthy cell membranes, growth, the development of sexual maturation and production, smell, taste, a functioning immune system, healthy sperm, wound healing, and many more functions. Zinc is found in every cell in the body; perhaps it is the most important mineral in the human body.

But, for our purposes, it is enough to know that zinc inhibits estrogen—and that is a good thing.

Factor Three: Obesity

Fat cells contribute to the build up of abdominal fat, which then, in turn, causes the formation of more estrogen, stimulating the enzyme aromatase, that turn testosterone into estrogen. Weight gain causes even lower levels of testosterone, which, in turn, causes even higher estrogen levels. In other words, you should do everything you can to fight obesity.

Factor Four: The Liver

The liver is an organ designed to clean the waste products out of the body. Estrogen is excreted, and it is eliminated through the liver. If the liver is not working properly, if liver function is impaired, then a surplus of estrogen is created. A healthy liver is extremely important to hormone balance. How does a liver get clogged? Well, with alcohol, unhealthy lifesyles (lack of exercise, over eating and permanent stress) and, most importantly, with the use of drugs. In other words, if you are taking drugs—prescription drugs—the liver cannot keep up, and the result is an imbalance of hormone levels.

Factor Five: Aromatase Enzyme

Enzymes are protein-like substances formed in plant and animal cells. They act as catalysts. They start or speed up specific chemical changes and turn certain substances into others. Sounds complicated? Okay, let's keep it simple. Special enzymes help to digest faster, better. They speed up the body process of turning food into substances the body can use. They change some chemicals, body chemicals. Enzymes are usually necessary. But, as men age, the body produces larger quantities of an enzyme called *aromatase,* and that is the problem. The aromatase enzyme converts testosterone into estrogen. So if you could inhibit this aromatase enzyme to convert testosterone into estrogen–then what? Yes, then you could end with the excess estrogen level. And remember: we want less estrogen and more testosterone.

In other words, a man older than thirty or fifty should do just that: balance out hormonal imbalances. He should do everything possible to make sure that the testosterone levels stay up and estrogen levels stay low.

Factor Six: DHT and Alpha Reductase Enzyme

Another enzyme that is a problem is the *alpha reductase enzyme.* Alpha reductase enzyme converts testosterone into DHT (Dihydrotestosterone). In other words, you need to keep very low levels of estrogen, especially estradiol, and low levels of DHT. You need, generally speaking, a correct balance of your hormones.

But what do I need to do exactly? You might ask.

Well, there are eleven steps, rungs that lead up this ladder called hormonal balance. We will talk about it in the next chapter, and then it gets really exciting.

First, let us quickly summarize what we have learned.

Action

Information: Hormones *excite and* give *impulses.* A hormone is a substance formed in an organ of the body (gland); this substance is then carried to another organ (or tissue), where it fulfills a specific purpose. Hormones are in careful balance with one another.

Action: Check to see if your hormone levels are balanced. Do a saliva test.

Information: Estrogen points at any female sex hormones. Estrogen is not one hormone; it is the name of a group of hormones. Estrone, estradiol, and estriol (E1, E2, and E3) are all estrogens.

Action: The higher the estrogen levels in men, the worse the repercussions. Get the estrogen levels down by natural means.

Information: Progesterone is a hormone.In women, it stimulates the uterus to prepare for pregnancy. In men, progesterone inhibits the harmful effects of excess estrogen.

Action: Use progesterone in a cream form regularly.

Information: Testosterone is relates to the male sex hormones produced by the testicles. When a man gets older, he produces less testosterone.

Action: Get the testosterone level up by natural means.

Information: DHT (Dihydrotestosterone) is a male hormone, and the main cause for the shrinking of the hair follicle and for hair loss. It can cause prostate enlargement and prostate cancer.

Action: A test will show you if you have the optimal amount of this hormone.

ACTION

Information: The golden formula for optimal hormonal balance is 60/200/1/1 of testosterone/progesterone/estradiol/DHT.
Action: If your hormones are not in optimal balance, you must *act*.

Information: During andropause (male menopause), the testosterone level is low. Testosterone has many functions: It is important for the brain and the heart; it improves oxygen intake, controls blood sugar, is important for the immune system and red blood cells, and more. Many studies indicate that testosterone does not cause prostate cancer. However, high levels of estradiol and high levels of DHT (Dihydrotestosterone) may cause prostate cancer.
Action: The prostate should be checked before taking additional testosterone. Taking testosterone can help avoid taking too many drugs, which can cause horrible side effects. Replace testosterone, but never overdo it. Always monitor the results of testosterone on your body with hormone saliva tests.

Information: Alcohol produces a dramatic estrogen-testosterone imbalance.
Action: Stay away from all types of alcohol.

Information: Zinc inhibits excess levels of estrogen.
Action: Take additional zinc.

Information: Fat cells start a vicious cycle, and, in the end, they lower the level of testosterone.
Action: Do everything you can to get slim, but don't take drugs.

Information: The liver is extremely important for the hormone balance. Alcohol, an unhealthy lifestyle, and drugs all clog the liver.

Action: Do everything you can to create a healthy lifestyle, stay away from alcohol and drugs, and you will succeed in cleaning your liver.

Information: The so-called *aromatase enzyme* converts testosterone into estrogen.
Action: After testing your homone levels, use natural aromatase inhibitors. (See the next chapter.)

Information: *The alpha reduction enzyme* converts testosterone into DHT.
Action: Use natural alpha reduction enzyme inhibitors. (See next chapter.)

IV.

Eleven Tools

Let us be poetic for a moment, and let us look for substances that do just that: Inhibit the *aromatase enzyme* that converts testosterone into estrogen. The old magicians did just that; they looked for substances that could possibly give us eternal life. Nearly every alchemist in the middle ages was not only driven by his urge to turn lead into gold but also to find some substance that would guarantee a longer life or even eternal life. Contrary to those old charlatans, magicians, and alchemists, today we can precisely measure which substances are doing what. There is no guessing anymore. Galileo Galilei stressed the triumph of exact measurement uncompromisingly—for the first time in history. That was the first milestone. The second milestone, one might say, is globalization. Research is done in Germany, France, South America, North America, Japan, and Russia. The results are at our fingertips. Carefully done worldwide research provides us with many tools that enable the body to do many things, such as: inhibit the aromatase enzyme and therefore inhibit the conversion of testosterone into estrogen. There is more good news. Those tools can do much more, and they are "natural." They exist in nature; they are not "drugs." So let us look at those tools that can prolong our lives and help us stay healthy.

Chrysyn

Chrysin is a *bioflavonoid*.

Again, not another new word, you might say. Sorry, it is necessary, but it is also simple. Bioflavonoids are a group of substances found in plants; they can strengthen the walls of capillaries (the tiny blood vessels connecting the arteries with the veins) and help prevent hemorrhaging (heavy bleeding). Bioflavonoids are present mainly in citrus fruits and black currants and were formerly considered a vitamin. Collectively, bioflavonoids are regarded as one vitamin: vitamin P. So the term *bioflavonoid* embraces all vitamin Ps (there are many sorts of vitamin P). One bioflavonoid is the famous chrysin.

What does chrysin do? Chrysin, which can be extracted from several plants, has shown potential as a natural Aromatase-inhibitor. The only problem with chrysin is that it is not easily absorbed into our blood-stream. But there is a solution to handle this problem: pepper extract (piperine). So when used with piperine, chrysin can be absorbed into our blood-stream. The result? Chrysin (combined with piperine) reduces estrogen and increases testosterone. Chrysin has the power to do that within thirty days. It is the most potent Aromatase-inhibitor known so far. It does exactly what scientists in the past were so desperately trying to work out when they gave their patients more testosterone, but this testosterone was converted into estrogen. The patient got worse, sicker, and older. We now know the body does not work that way. We cannot just administer what it is lacking. The body is an extremely fine-tuned biochemical machine that only functions well if its original mechanisms are obeyed.

Anyway, the good news is that chrysin at a daily dose of 1500 to 2000 mg can naturally suppress excess estrogen and boost testosterone at the same time. Now allow us to let you in on a little secret: nobody in the pharmaceutical industry is interested in promoting chrysin. Why? It is not a patentable drug. No big money can be made with chrysin. There is no economic potential. But many people who want to do something against aging prefer natural resources. They don't want another drug. They accept taking vitamins and natural supplements, but not drugs. We are fans of natural sources, too. Natural chrysin also has other benefits. It has anti-inflammatory effects, so chronic inflammation can be inhibited or reduced by chrysin. It can even protect against atherosclerosis, senility, aortic problems, and some sorts of cancer. It also has anti-anxiety and relaxing effects on the brain., All this makes chrysin pure gold. Yes, it is like having turned lead into gold, but without any side effects. For our purposes, it is important to remember that chrysin is an inhibitor of estrogen, that it boosts testosterone, and that it has several other positive effects. Why obsessively change nature and try to come up with a "chemical" similar to chrysin?

Nettle-Root

Even if you start hating us, we have to bother you with some more theory. The testicles produce about 90 percent of male testosterone, and the remainder is produced by the adrenal glands. There are two types of testosterone in our bodies, *free testosterone* and *bound testosterone*. What is the difference? Well, there is another hormone (SHBG) that binds to testosterone so that it becomes biologically inactive. Bound testosterone is not as interesting as free testosterone precisely because it is inactive. We want to learn about the testosterone that can do something. This other hormone, which binds testosterone, is called SHBG (Sex Hormone Binding Globulin), and we have already talked about it. SHBG increases at the age of forty by about 40 percent. By the way, the number of new words a medical student has to learn is equivalent to learning how to fluently speak five languages. In males, SHBG has a particularly high affinity to testosterone and Dihydrotestosterone (DHT) to which it binds up to 98 percent.

What a horrible fact. So if you're just taking artificial testosterone, it is not only converted to estrogen, it is also bound by that "evil" hormone and is not available to your cells, so it cannot be absorbed by your body. Additionally, the liver isn't building testosterone. And if you use sedatives, tranquilizers, alcoholic beverages—in short, any sort of drug—then this situation is worsened. People usually take the horrible drugs to "help" themselves, prescription drugs like beta-blockers, anti-depressants, etc. The result is a vicious cycle. A downward spiral starts. Side effects have to be handled.

That's the bad news. Here comes the good news. There is a plant called nettle; some may have heard of it. It has jagged leaves covered with stinging hairs. In Germany, where it originated, it is called *nessel*. Now here comes the kicker: nettle root can bind to SHBG (the evil hormone that inactivates testosterone) decreasing its bioavailability. There is less SHBG available to bind with testosterone, so there is more unbound (active) testosterone. In other words, it decreases the negative effects of this bad hormone. What is the result? Well, we have our second tool that points in the right direction, and it is all natural. By the way, even the prostate benefits from nettle root. In Germany, prostate enlargement has been successfully treated with nettle root for the last ten years. So here again, this plant has other positive effects, unlike drugs.

DIM (Di-Indolyl Methane)

As we continue in our quest for an optimal hormonal balance, we encounter DIM. DIM (Di-Indolyl Methane) is a natural ingredient found in cruciferous vegetables, such as broccoli, cabbage, cauliflower, and brussels sprouts, which promotes a beneficial estrogen metabolism in both men and women.

Now let us differentiate between "good" estrogen and "bad" estrogen. The "bad" estrogen may be responsible for prostate cancer, uterine cancer, breast cancer, and ovarian cancer. Supplementing the diet with DIM and eating cruciferous vegetables increases the chances for estrogen to be broken down into its beneficial or "good" estrogen metabolites. Many of the benefits that are attributed to estrogen, such as its ability to protect the heart and brain with its antioxidant activity, are now known to come from these "good" metabolites.

But what is a *metabolite*? And what is the exact definition of the word *metabolism*?

Well, *metabolism* is the sum of all the chemical and physical changes that take place within the body and enable its continued growth and function. Metabolism is the process of cells burning food to produce energy. This process is similar to a car's engine burning gasoline to produce the energy that is needed to rotate the car's wheels. The food we eat acts as the gasoline, and the energy we need to move and think is similar to the energy used to move the car. Metabolism is also referred to as *energy metabolism*. Metabolites are substances that are used by or produced by enzyme reactions.

Back to our original thought. When DIM increases the "good" estrogen, there is a simultaneous reduction in the levels of undesirable or "bad" estrogen. Greater production of these "bad" estrogen metabolites is promoted by obesity and exposure to a number of man-made environmental chemicals. These "bad" estrogen metabolites are responsible for many of estrogen's undesirable actions in women and men, including further unwanted weight gain, breast cancer, uterine cancer, and prostate cancer.

Androstenedione

We already introduced a new hormone in the last chapter. Its name is *androstenedione*. But now let us look deeper into it. Androstenedione, also known as "Andro," is a hormone found in all animals and some plants. It can be converted into testosterone, the principle male sex hormone. *Androstenedione* is produced in the gonads (*gonads* are ovaries and testes) and adrenal glands and is required for the growth and maturation of the male sex organs. It also stimulates the growth of muscles and is used by athletes to enhance their athletic performance. Many males are taking *andro* as a testosterone therapy to stimulate and restore libido, increase energy, vitality, and a general sense of well-being. *Andro* is safer and far less expensive than testosterone treatments. *Andro* is converted into natural testosterone by the liver. Today, weight lifters, body builders, and other athletes are using *andro* to enhance their performance. It is not recommended that a male take more than 100 mg day. This is a powerful hormone, and its abuse can lead to exaggerated testosterone levels and aggressive behavior. Males over thirty-five years of age should take 50 mg of *andro* once a day to maintain their testosterone at youthful levels. In older men, this use will lead to increased sexual performance, vitality, energy, and a general feeling of restored youth. It is strongly recommended that andro supplements be accompanied by periodic saliva hormone tests to insure that proper levels are maintained and the recommended hormone levels are not exceeded. It is also recommended that you monitor estrogen (estradiol) levels to be sure they are not increasing.

Progesterone

We already introduced this hormone. The first thing we need to understand is that men and women have exactly the same hormones-only in different amounts. Women have testosterone and androstenedione as well. Men have estriol, estrone, estradiol, progesterone, luteinizing hormone (LH), and follicle-stimulating hormone (FSH).

Luteinizing hormone (LH) is a hormone secreted by the pituitary gland in brain that stimulates the growth and maturation of eggs in females and sperm in males.

The follicle-stimulating hormone (FSH) is a hormone secreted by the pituitary gland in the brain that stimulates the growth and maturation of eggs in females, sperm in males, and produces sex hormones in both males and females.

These two hormones are secreted from cells in the anterior pituitary. As men age, their levels of estrogen rise—especially the two most dangerous and potent estrogens, *estrone* and *estradiol*. A man over fifty literally has more estrogen than his postmenopausal wife. It is finally becoming clear that this excess of estrogen in aging men is responsible for a variety of problems, such as adiposity, breast development, many cancers, prostate problems, baldness, and other problems that come with advanced age.

Now what is the most potent antagonist of estrogen? Progesterone. It is progesterone that inhibits those harmful effects of excess estrogen more than anything else. As estrogen levels rise in men, there is no parallel rise in progesterone. Any man over fifty may well choose to use a small amount of *transdermal* natural progesterone daily to offset the excess estrogens in his blood. (*Trans* = through, *derma* = skin. The substance goes through the skin and will end up in the bloodstream. It refers to creams, ointments, or other substances applied directly to the skin). Women commonly use about 24 mg; a man could use 12 mg a day. It is reassuring to know that progesterone has no toxicity, especially in these small amounts. It is very safe to use without any known side effects. Studies in laboratory animals given very large doses resulted in no side effects.

DHEA (Dehydroepiandrosterone)

DHEA (Dehydroepiandrosterone) is a hormone produced in our body by the adrenal glands. We already talked about it in the last chapter. The adrenal glands are orange-colored endocrine glands, which are located on top of both kidneys. The adrenal glands are triangular shaped and measure about one-half inch in height and three inches in length.

So what are the benefits of taking DHEA? In short, it increases energy, increases libido, increases muscle strength and endurance, lowers cholesterol, improves memory, strengthens the immune system, facilitates weight loss, maintains bone density, increases resistance to stress, and has anti-depressant effects. DHEA can be converted to testosterone by the body, and it promotes the balanced production of other hormones. Not Bad.

Pregnenolone

We will never stop apologizing for introducing new hormones. The next one is called *Pregnenolone*. Just take it as another word. What are the benefits of pregnenolone? Well, it is the most potent memory enhancer, it facilitates learning, it helps us adapt to stress, it improves concentration, it prevents mental fatigue, it increases productivity, and it helps prevent depression.

Eurycoma Longifolia Jack

Eurycoma longifolia jack, commonly known as *tongkat ali* in Malaysia and *pask bumi* in Indonesia, is a wild scrub tree found along the hilly slopes of the rainforest of Malaysia and other parts of Southeast Asia. The primary benefits of eurycoma longifolia jack are: that it improves testosterone production and physical and mental performance; it enhances energy level, endurance, and stamina; it reduces mental fatigue and exhaustion; and it improves skin tone, muscle, and the immune system.

Tribulus Terrestris

Tribulus terrestris is not a hormone. It is a plant extract and works very differently than andro. Tribulus terrestris increases testosterone by increasing luteinizing hormone (LH) in one's body. LH sends a signal to the testicles to produce more testosterone.

Maca, Lepidium Meyenii G

Peruvian maca root cultivation goes back perhaps five millennia. maca was an integral part of the diet and commerce of residents of the Andes region. The Incas found maca root so potent that they restricted maca use to royalty. Colonial Spaniards became aware of maca's value and collected tribute in Peruvian maca for export. The Spanish royalty also used maca root as an energy enhancer and as food. Eventually, knowledge of maca's special qualities died out, and maca was preserved only in remote Peruvian communities. In the 1960s and 80s, Peruvian Gloria Chacon, who was researching botanicals in Peru, rekindled interest in Peruvian maca through nutritional analysis of what was designated as "the lost crops of the Andes." The publication of a book by that name introduces maca root to the world. Peruvian maca was one of the first plants to be domesticated by the Andean people. Maca cultivation continued during the colonial times until the sixteenth century, and maca's importance gradually varied throughout the years. Maca was known to have been used a nutrient and medicine for two thousand years. What are the benefits of maca root for men? Maca root enhances aphrodisiac activity (sexual drive and desire), increases energy, stamina, and endurance, improves male potency, helps with depression, helps in the treatment of stress, and increases sperm count. In addition, it improves athletic performance, balances hormones, increases testosterone levels, helps with erectile dysfunction, and is good for fertility enhancement.

Muira Puama

French scientists sing the song of praise to this herbal extract. *Muira puama* is won from the stems and roots of a plant called ptychopetalum olacoides. You better forget that word fast. This plant is very well known in the Amazon region of South America. Muira puama can help in many ways. It is said to cure rheumatism, muscle problems, sexual dysfunction, and stomach problems.

Again, what we are interested in is the testosterone level. Quite a few studies have shown that the sexual function is better after taking muira puama, which seems to indicate that it does something good for our hormonal balance. We don't know yet exactly how this plant works, sometimes nature keeps its secrets jealously, but we know that it does increase libido. So this is an important weapon in our fight for testosterone.

Testosterone Cream

Another way to replace testosterone is by using testosterone cream. But you need a prescription to get testosterone cream from a compound pharmacy.

So there is a lot you can do.

Testing

Hurrah! You might say, "Now I know the secret for a longer life. Now I am smarter than all those drug companies, the whole pharmaceutical industry, the doctors, the old alchemist, and the magicians." Well, you know something, yes. There is a big *but,* though. With age, all sorts of *specific* problems arise. So it is not wise to leave out testing. The first step when you want to re-balance your hormones is to take some tests first. The good news is there are supplements used today that boost free testosterone, suppress excess estrogen, and balance out the hormones. You just read about them. Yes, you can use these supplements, but we recommend you *test* your hormone levels before starting and monitor your results closely. If only for one reason—each human body is unique.

In no case should you just go and buy any synthetic or even natural testosterone products. You should not follow our "eleven tools" and think all will be better. No, do a test first. The best and most cost-effective way to test is with a saliva test. You can test at home and send the sample in by mail. It is very accurate and will measure only the free hormone. The cost is very low, and you don't need a doctor's prescription. You need to measure free, or unbound, hormones because they are the ones that are acting in your cells. You do not want to test hormones that are bound to transport proteins, because these hormones are inactive. If your doctor wants to take a *blood hormone test,* be sure it measures *free* hormones. These tests cost much more than saliva tests.

The following hormones can be measured in saliva: testosterone, estrogen (estradiol, estriol, estrone), progesterone, pregnenolone, and DHEA. Some hormones cannot be measured in saliva yet, so sometimes blood tests are necessary.

Are all these tests really necessary? Yes. Again, if you show signs of prostate cancer, it could be deadly increasing your estradiol and DHT levels. And you have to establish the *exact amount* that you should take. Any testosterone replacement therapy must be accompanied by a special saliva test, a digital rectal examination, and a PSA test so that prostate cancer is ruled out. Again, you don't want to have high levels of estradiol and DHT when prostrate cancer is present, because prostate cancer cells grow better and faster in the presence of estradiol and DHT.

In general, when you replace hormones, some good advice is to never overdo it; you want to restore your hormones to their youthful levels but not more. Like everything in life, not too much, not too little, just the right amount is correct. Balance is the key.

So let us summarize quickly what we already know before we attack a more specific problem that, inevitably relates to men when they age: the decline of the prostate.

Action

There are eleven tools to balance out your hormones.

Information: Chrysin is a bioflavonoid. Bioflavonoids are regarded as vitamin Ps.

Action: Extracted chrysin along with pepper extract (piperine) reduces estrogen and increases testosterone. A daily dose of 1500 to 2000 mg can naturally suppress excess estrogen and boost low testosterone.

Information: Nettle root binds to a hormone that usually binds to testosterone, thus increasing free testosterone.

Action: Use 300 mg natural nettle roots a day (after testing).

Information: DIM (Di-Indolyl Methane) is a natural ingredient found in cruciferous vegetables which increases the beneficial estrogen metabolism.

Action: Use 200 mg of DIM (Di-Indolyl Methane) daily.

Information: Androstendione, or simply known as "andro," is a hormone found in all animals and some plants. It serves as a direct precursor of testosterone.

Action: Use 50 to 100 mg of androstendione a day. Always monitor your estradiol and testosterone levels with saliva tests.

Information: The most potent antagonist to estrogen is progesterone. It is progesterone that inhibits those harmful effects of excess estrogen. As estrogen levels rise in men, there is no parallel rise in progesterone.

Action: Any man over forty may well choose to use a small amount of transdermal natural progesterone daily to offset the excess estrogens in his blood. Since women commonly use about 24 mg, a man could use 12 mg a day.

Information: As we age, DHEA decreases dramatically.
Action: Use 25 to 50 mg of DHEA a day orally or 12 mg a day in a transdermal cream.

Information: Pregnenolone is the most potent memory and mental enhancer.
Action: Take 50 mg of pregnenolone a day orally or 12 mg a day in a transdermal cream.

Information: Eurycoma longifolia jack improves testosterone production and physical and mental performance; enhances energy levels, endurance, and stamina; and reduces mental fatigue, exhaustion, and more.
Action: Take 200 to 800 mg of eurycoma longifolia jack daily.

Information: Tribulus terrestris increases testosterone through luteinizing hormone (LH) in one's body. LH sends a signal to the testicles to produce testosterone.
Action: Take 400 mg of Tribulus terrestris daily.
Information: The benefits of maca for men: include aphrodisiac activity, enhanced libido, increased energy, stamina, and endurance, improved male potency, and helps in overcoming depression. DHEA levels increase significantly in the majority of the men treated. It helps in the treatment of stress, increases sperm count and athletic performance, balances hormones, increases testosterone levels, and helps with erectile dysfunction and fertility enhancement.
Action: Use 300 mg of maca daily.

Information: Muira puama helps improve libido.
Action: Take 300 mg of miura puama daily

Information: Testosterone cream can increase testosterone levels.

Action: It may be used, but you need a prescription from a doctor. Always test first.

Saliva testing is the most cost-effective way to monitor your hormone levels (testosterone, estradiol, progesterone, DHT, pregnenolone, and DHEA).

V.

Prostate Problems

The last chapter contains general information. And yes, it may not be specific enough for the problem you might have. So when we want to fight aging effectively, we must go far more into detail.

The reason for this is obvious.

Aging has a lot to do with the sexual functions. So let us jump into our first subject: prostate health.

Let us first consider some facts that are indisputable.

Most men don't know that they even *have* a prostate until one day they realize one or more of the following:

- Blood in the urine
- Pain while urinating
- Infections in the genitals
- Problems with intercourse
    (pain, odd sensations, blood in semen)
- Premature ejaculation (often)
- Avoiding intercourse
- Urination stream is thin
- Urination stream stops halfway
- Bladder does not empty completely
- Frequent urination at night or during the day
- Losing urine

While none of these symptoms necessarily mean that there is a serious problem, when some of these indicators are present, there may be a prostate problem. If these symptoms exist, it is wise to act fast.

When a doctor encounters the prostate subject with patients, he or she usually has to first clear up the word itself. In other words, one must know what the prostate is. Well, the prostate is a little gland (actually it is a combination of several glands) with an outer shell, resembling a walnut or a chestnut. It is located under the bladder, and you could look at it as a little factory that is necessary for some of the production of your semen. There may be other functions as well, but this is the main function. A picture may give you an idea of its location.

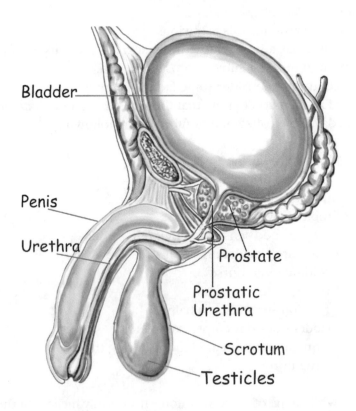

Illustration of the anatomy of the prostate

So again, the prostate is located under the bladder and above the testicles, and it assists in the ejaculation process.

The cycle is simple: sperm is produced in the testicles, and the sperm moves finally to the muscle tissue through the *ductus deferens* and through some other stations until it winds up in the prostate, the last station before it moves out of the body. How does the semen move out? The muscles in the ductus deferens, the prostate, and the penis contract. It's simple.

In other words, the main function of the prostate consists of producing a fluid, that is mixed with the sperm for ejaculation purposes. The force with which the semen comes out of the body is another function of the prostate. So the prostate is both a gland and a muscle. Here are some more facts: The prostate size increases with age. At birth, it weighs just a few grams. Between the ages of twenty and fifty-five, the prostate weighs about twenty grams. After that the prostate grows.

Now let us define the prostate in the frame of reference of hormones. In fact, prostate growth is *hormonally* regulated. The cycle is as follows:

1. Testosterone converts to Dihydrotestosterone.
2. Dihydrotestosterone stimulates prostate growth.
3. Estrogen also stimulates prostate growth.

We do not need to again explain the exact purpose of those hormones. In short, these hormones are responsible for the growth of the prostate.

Three Problems

Generally speaking (and intentionally simplified), there are three main problems, three things that can go wrong, with the prostate:
1. Prostatitis (also called prostate infections)
2. Prostate enlargement (BPH)

3. Prostate cancer

The symptoms of infections in the prostate include pain while urinating, and pain during intercourse. Prostatitis may account for up to 25 percent of all young and middle-aged men's urology consults. Some people can have these symptoms for many years. We will talk about that later.

The enlargement of the prostate (also called benign prostate hypertrophy and benign prostate hyperplasia, in short, BPH) isn't nice at all, but it has nothing to do with cancer. About half of all men sixty years of age have BPH, and so do about 90 percent of all men of eighty years of age, according to the National Institute of Health.

The likelihood of developing an enlarged prostate increases with age. In fact, BPH is so common that it has been said "all men will have an enlarged prostate if they live long enough. A small amount of prostate enlargement is present in many men over age forty and more than 90 percent of men over age eighty.

Some symptoms include the following: the enlarged prostate presses the urethra causing urine to come too late, problems starting to urinate, thin, weak urine, and other similar problems. At night, you may have to get out of bed continuously, perhaps you can't empty your bladder fully anymore, or, worse, you are unable to hold back the urine.

It is not as problematic as it may seem at first glance; many medical and even alternative healing solutions exist.

The third problem, *cancer* is, of course, the toughest one. But even here there is good news. Anti-aging medicine provides quite a lot of technologies to prevent cancer problems from developing in the first place.

These are the three major problems of the prostate. Now let us look at each of these three problems a little bit closer.

Prostatitis

If you encounter a medical term ending with *itis,* know it refers to inflammation or swelling. Tonsillitis is an inflammation or swelling of the tonsils; prostatitis is an inflammation or swelling of the prostate. There are four types of prostatitis: acute bacterial, chronic bacterial, nonbacterial inflammation, and prostatodynia, which is caused by muscle spasms. Let us take a closer look:

- Acute bacterial prostatitis: The symptoms include fever, chills, pain in the lower back, pain between rectum and testicles, painful urination, urgent need to urinate, and blood in the urine.
- You are more likely to get acute bacterial prostatitis if you have any of the following:
- Obstruction to the flow of urine so that it backs up and becomes infected
- Prostate enlargement
- A prostate tumor
- A urinary catheter inserted into the urethra
- A sexually transmitted disease such as gonorrhea
- Anal and oral sex
- A suppressed immune system
- A bladder infection
- Diabetes

The treatment is relatively simple: antibiotics, anti-inflammatory immune boosters, and thermotherapy will do.

Of course, it is a better idea to use natural supplements to reduce inflammation and to boost the immune system.

But what can you do?

Well, you can take *quercetin,* for example. Quercetin is a bioflavonoid that reduces inflammation.

Quercetin is a natural anti-inflammatory that can work

very well in the prostate at 1500 mg a day. Quercetin may be the strongest of nature's anti-inflammatories. Numerous studies have shown it is effective in treating a wide range of prostate-related problems.

A recent published study demonstrates quercetin provides long-term symptomatic relief with few side effects to men who are afflicted with nonbacterial prostatitis. Quercetin is an *anti-oxidant* and has been shown to reduce the risks associated with high cholesterol levels. (An antioxidant is a molecule that is capable of reacting with *free radicals* and neutralizing them. Free radicals are atoms or molecules that are highly reactive with other cellular structures because they contain unpaired electrons; free radicals can be very harmful to cells.) Quercetin gives, by the way, red and rose wines their distinctive color and may be the reason men who drink red and rose wines appear to have a lower incidence of prostate problems.

Pollen flower extract is another alternative. In simple terms, pollen flower extract consists of the male germ seeds of plants, and as such plays a vital role in ensuring that plant life in the world continues.

Pollen contains all other essential substances, such as fat, vitamins, minerals, hormones, enzymes, and co-enzymes. (Co-enzymes are small molecules, not proteins but sometimes vitamins, essential for the activity of some enzymes.) Therefore, pollen is essential for the survival of the bees in the hive. If too much pollen was removed from any particular hive, the unfortunate colony would surely die. There is no substitute that man has devised to replace pollen, it is the bee's protein, body, and life.

It had been known for generations that a grain of pollen, minute as it is, holds all the elements of plant life: vitamins, minerals, hormones, and nucleic acids. Like honey and royal jelly, pollen contains certain elements that still defy identification. It was a long time before man was able to find a way of piercing these tiny grains. Pollen has baffled us for years, and it will take much more research before all the secrets are known.

Let us now take a close look at our problem: chronic prostatitis.

Since 1957, pollen has been extensively used as a tonic in Sweden. During this long period, it has been proven effective for patients convalescing from operations or illnesses, and there have been no side effects reported. In 1960, a Swedish specialist, Dr. E. Ask-Upmark, Department of Medicine, University Hospital, Uppsala, issued reports that pollen was effective to treat chronic prostatitis. This is a fairly common genital disease affecting males, which often proves difficult to treat. Two years later, a Swedish specialist, Dr. Leander, used pollen to treat one hundred cases of chronic prostatitis, and nearly 80 percent achieved remission. In 1967, Dr. Ask-Upmark reported twelve patients suffering from this illness who were again treated with pollen, and ten were completely cured. Other experts have confirmed the findings of these Swedish specialists. In East Germany, Professor Helse endorsed the opinions of the Swedish doctors. Danish expert Professor Heise did likewise and added that pollen had quickly cured male patients suffering from various sexual problems. Pollen had proved to be effective in many cases where orthodox treatment was not only prolonged, but also doomed to fail. In East Berlin, three-year trials were conducted on males suffering from impotence, other sexual disorders, and chronic prostatitis. Many had a complete cure and were once again able to enjoy normal sexual relations. Others recovered from prostatitis, which had failed to respond to various kinds of treatment.

Borage Oil

Borage oil is another possibility to treat prostatitis. Borage oil is derived from the seeds of the borage (borago officinalis) plant. The large plant with blue, star-shaped flowers is found throughout Europe and North Africa. It is natural to North America.

Borage oil, evening primrose oil, and *black currant seed oil* contain compounds that the body converts to a hormone-like substance called prostaglandin E1 (PGE1). PGE1 has anti-inflammatory properties and also may act as a blood thinner and blood vessel dilator.

But many things can interfere with this conversion, including disease, the aging process, saturated fats, hydrogenated oils, blood sugar problems, inadequate vitamin C intake, magnesium, zinc, and B vitamin deficiencies. Supplements that provide specific elements circumvent these conversion problems, leading to more predictable formation of PGE1.

Evening Primrose Oil

Evening primrose oil is made from a plant that is rich in a substance that's biologically important to our bodies. Poor skin condition, eczema, susceptibility to infections, and inappropriate wound healing can be associated with a lack of this substance. Evening primrose oil provides the body with a rich source of oil that supports the body's cardiovascular, nervous, immune, and reproductive systems. *Cardiovascular* means related to heart and blood vessels.

Evening primrose oil enhances the health and strength of cell membranes throughout the body and promotes a proper inflammatory response. Evening primrose oil also helps maintain healthy hormone levels.

Beta Glucan / IP6
Beta Glucan and IP6 boost the immune system.
Prostatic Massage

One of the causes of pain in prostatitis is the build-up of pressure in the prostate due to an accumulation of semen or fluids from bacterial infection. One way to relieve the pressure is to have the prostate massaged. A doctor can insert a gloved finger into the rectum and use firm pressure to force the excess products from the prostate. This procedure can be somewhat painful; however, relieving the pressure can relieve pain for a longer period of time. Prostatic massage is a simple procedure; it may be done by a person who is not a physician. Sometimes the patient is advised to have sex with ejaculation at least two to three times a week to relieve built-up pressure.

Thermotherapy

A last resort for prostatitis is *thermotherapy*. Thermotherapy is a therapy using heat. With the use of heat, we can treat diseases or disorders. Thermotherapy is controlled by a microprocessor that heats a temperature probe. This temperature probe, also called a rectal probe, is in the shape of an elongated *suppository*. It is inserted into the anal canal. A suppository is a small plug of medication designed for insertion into the rectum or vagina where it melts. While using the probe, the patient can adjust the temperature in the probe to a comfortable level of 99° F -to 113° F (37° C-45° C). The probe radiates pulsating heat waves for twenty-minute periods. This daily therapy eases pain and reduces swelling. According to studies done in Europe, after eight sessions, 85 percent of patients with prostatitis feel improvement. (For patients with BPH, 82 percent feel improvement after six weeks.)

- **Chronic bacterial:** The symptoms include long-lasting or recurring infections, painful urination, pain in the pelvis and genital areas, frequent, difficult urination, and urgent need to urinate.

  Again the treatment is relatively simple: antibiotics, anti-inflammatory, pollen flower, immune boosters, and thermotherapy.

- **Nonbacterial:** The symptoms include painful urination, and pain in the lower back, penis, scrotum, etc.

  The treatment is a bit more sophisticated, since the source is unknown. Frequent hot baths, anti-inflammatory medication, and a change in diet may help. For sure you should no't drink alcohol or coffee. Altogether it is still something you can deal with relatively easily; there is no reason to panic.

- **Prostatodynia** is an inflammation caused by muscle spasms. The symptoms include painful or frequent urination, and pain in the lower back, penis, scrotum, etc. It gets treated like nonbacterial prostatitis. Although we do not have to worry too much about prostatitis, any man can get it whether he is young or old. Sometimes lifestyle changes, no alcohol, no coffee, etc. are necessary to avoid it. Anti-inflammatory, medication, pollen flower, immune boosters, and thermotherapy can do the job. The stronger the body, the better the immune system can fight bacteria. But prostatitis is usually not at all dangerous; it won't stop one from getting to be one hundred twenty years old.

BPH

Urologists differentiate between *benign prostatic hyperplasia and benign prostatic hypertrophy. Hypertrophy* means the actual size of the prostate is bigger, while *hyperplasia* shows that the number of prostate cells has increased. The term *benign* points to a medical condition generally favorable for recovery. *Benign* means non-cancerous, non-malignant, not permanently damaging. Actually the term *benign prostate hypertrophy* is an older expression; more modern is *benign prostatic hyperplasia.* Both terms refer to the growth of a benign tumor inside the prostate today. Some-times these two terms are used parallel without differentiation. Again, BPH has no relation to cancer.

But the hard-hitting fact is this: one in six men (7 percent) between the ages forty and fifty years of age, one in four men (25 percent) between the ages fifty and sixty years, and one in every two men over the age of sixty will have BPH. In other words, BPH is very frequent. Hormonal imbalances will cause it. Still, there is no reason to panic.

The only thing that may be uncomfortable is that an enlarged prostate can put pressure on the urethra, resulting in urinary problems. An individual can detect BPH by himself, by watching for these urinary symptoms:

- Weak urine flow
- The inability to empty the bladder completely
- The inability to urinate at all
- Difficulty in holding one's urine or the need to urinate immediately
- Interrupted sleep due to the constant need to urinate at night
- Wetting or staining of underwear

Those urinary problems do not automatically indicate the presence of BPH, because urinary difficulties can signify a wide variety of conditions, but they do point toward it. When you go to the doctor, it is likely you will be asked to fill out a questionnaire developed by the American Urological Association. The questionnaire will inquire about your ability (or inability) to urinate in the past month. The doctor will use your answers to develop a "symptom score" to determine the severity of the problem.

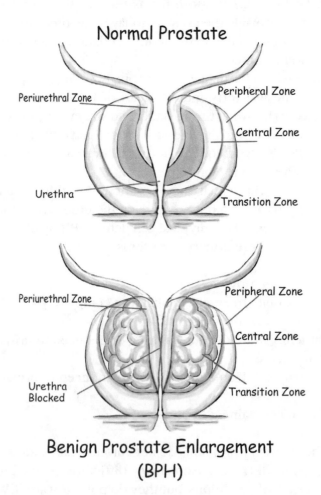

Normal Prostate

Periurethral Zone

Peripheral Zone

Central Zone

Urethra

Transition Zone

Periurethral Zone

Peripheral Zone

Central Zone

Urethra Blocked

Transition Zone

Benign Prostate Enlargement (BPH)

This illustration shows a normal prostate with an open urethra and a BPH- enlarged prostate with the urethra blocked.

This is what the questionnaire looks like:

1. During the past month or so, how often have you had a sensation of not emptying your bladder completely after you've finished urinating?
2. During the past month or so, how often have you had to urinate again in less then two hours after you've finished urinating?
3. During the past month or so, how often have you found you stopped and started again several times when you urinated?
4. During the last month or so, how often have you found it difficult to postpone urination?
5. During the past month or so, how long have you had a weak urinary stream?
6. During the past month or so, how often have you had to push or strain to begin urination?
7. During the past month or so, how many times do you typically get up to urinate from the time you went to bed at night until the time you got up in the morning?

Scoring for Possible Answers to Questions 1 – 6
0 = Not at all
1 = Less than one time in five
2 = Less than half the time
3 = about half the time
4 = More than half the time
5 = Almost always
Symptom Score

Scoring for Possible Answers Question 7
0 = Not at all
1 = One time
2 = Two times
3 = Three times
4 = Four times
5 = Five times
(Sum of the Answers)

If you score 0-7, that means your symptoms are mild, 8-18 indicates your problem is moderate, and 19-35 means your symptoms are severe. Your treatment options will be based on your overall symptoms.

Prostate enlargement occurs in three stages:

Stage 1: The So-called Sensitivity Stage

The first noticeable symptoms are: an increased desire to urinate, the urinary stream is weaker and thin, and frequent passing of small amounts of urine (also during the night) is experienced. It is, however, still possible to empty the bladder almost completely. The first stage can continue over a number of years and, in some cases, it never progresses into the second stage.

Stage 2

It is no longer possible to empty the bladder completely. Quite often residue, amounting to more than 100 ml, will remain behind in the bladder. This result in a frequent and irritating desire to urinate without the relief associated with normal urination.

Stage 3

The urethra has become so narrow that normal urination is no longer possible. The *urethra* is a thin tube that carries urine from the bladder out of the body. The bladder now has to hold up to three liters of urine, and the pressure within the bladder increases considerably. For this reason, drops of urine are passed continually. The urine also is forced back into the upper urinary tract and then into the kidneys. This results in less-effective kidney function and will finally lead to renal failure.

Now, if it were necessary, you would need to take some additional tests:

- A digital rectal exam (DRE): helps to determine the size of the prostate and rules out prostate cancer.
- A urine test.
- A PSA (prostate specific antigen), which is a blood test to check BPH and cancer.

There may be more tests, but BPH is usually nothing to worry about. And again, it is frequent and age-related. The good news is that there are many treatment options today for BPH. There are a whole battery of natural therapies that exist. Yes, there also is the possibility of medical treatments (with alpha-blockers, etc.) or minimally invasive treatments (laser to electrical, from low level *radio-frequency* energy to surgery), all aimed to destroy prostate tissue. *Radio frequency* points at a form of energy that is used to ablate, or destroy, tissue. Some can be done with local anesthesia, some with general anesthesia. Surgical treatments also are possible. Prostatectomy (the surgical removal of the prostate) is still the most common treatment in cases of (heavy) BPH. Medical treatment is the second most common type of treatment.

But let us look at the alternatives to surgery.

Transurethral Microwave Thermotheraphy (TUMT)

Trans-rectal ultrasound is a procedure using ultrasound through the rectum to see the prostate.

Ultrasound is a diagnostic imaging technique that uses high-frequency sound waves and a computer to create images of blood vessels, tissues, and organs. Ultrasounds are used to view internal organs as they function and to assess blood flow through various vessels.

TUMT seems to be a good alternative to surgery. If prostate cells are subjected to temperatures of about 45∞ C-or 113∞ F-they will die. The source of hyperthermia is high-frequency microwaves similar to those used in home microwave cooking ovens. The microwave instrument systems are designed so that the temperature and the depth of heating are exactly controlled.

TUMT appears to offer very good results. The procedure offers an alternative for those men who are not good candidates for surgery.

Transurethral Needle Ablation (TUNA)

TUNA uses a low-level radiofrequency (RF) of about 490 kHz to create a temperature of 50--90∞ C in the area to be ablated. The probe is a special catheter that has two flexible needles at the tip. The needles are deployed and inserted into the prostate through the urethra. The needles are about 45 degrees apart. They are shielded at their base so that urethral tissue is not damaged. When the RF energy is turned on, it passes from one needle to the other so that prostatic tissue between the needles is destroyed. A transrectal ultrasound (TRUS) can view the progress of the treatment. The needles can be repositioned so that many areas of the prostate can be treated. The treatment can be an outpatient procedure with local anesthesia. The patient can leave soon after the treatment.

High-Intensity Focused Ultrasound (HIFU)

High-intensity focused ultrasound (HIFU) is being used to treat BPH, prostate cancer, and several other cancers. A special rectal ultrasound probe is used to treat BPH and prostate cancer. HIFU ablates benign prostatic tissue in a minimally invasive manner with low morbidity. HIFU has also been successfully used to treat localized prostate cancer and other tumors.

If you decide on an operation, we can only give you this advice: do not believe a doctor who says you have to act fast. No, wait and think. Get a second opinion. Read about your options and make up your own mind. Consider the natural treatments first, because a lot can be done.

Natural Treatments

Let us repeat: if you are diagnosed today with BPH, there is no need for fear. There are very powerful natural supplements today that can be used in cases of BPH. Let's talk about them.

Saw Palmetto

One of the most efficient alternatives to treat BPH is *saw palmetto*. What is saw palmetto? Saw palmetto is a wonder of nature. Saw palmetto is a berry that grows on dwarf-type palm trees. The botanical names are *serenoa repens (bartram) small,* but common names are *saw palmetto, American dwarf palm tree, cabbage palm, or sabal.* Saw palmetto grows wild in Texas, Louisiana, the Carolinas, Georgia, and Florida. Florida's pre-Columbian people and Native Americans used saw palmetto. There are more than twenty-nine published studies about saw palmetto, demonstrating the scientific effects in case of urinary tract symptoms and benign prostatic hyperplasia (BPH).

These are the effects of saw palmetto on the body:

- Reduced nocturnal urinary urgency
- Increased urinary flow rate
- Decreased urine volume in the bladder
- Reduceduncomfortable urination symptoms
- Reduced size of the prostate
- Balanced hormones
- Smoothed muscle contractions
- Reduced bladder size
- Elimination of aged prostate cells
- Anti-inflammatory effect on prostate tissue

In traditional folk medicine, saw palmetto has even been used to strengthen the whole reproductive system. So far, the reason why saw palmetto works so well has not been determined, but the effects are clinically documented. Of course, you have to watch what dose of saw palmetto you take. There are fluid extracts, aromatic oils, fixed fat oils, tinctures, and teas. The best source of saw palmetto and the correct amount has to be established if there is a BPH problem.

Beware, there are saw palmetto- products that hardly work and products that work excellently. In other words, you have to take the best quality saw palmetto product available.

So what is the optimal saw palmetto?

Supercritical fluid extraction technology today produces an extract of extraordinary purity, leaving behind no solvent residues on the product. The process uses carbon dioxide (CO_2) in its supercritical fluid state, when it is neither liquid nor gas.

Carbon dioxide is a colorless, odorless, incombustible gas. CO_2 is formed during respiration, combustion, and organic decomposition and is used in food refrigeration, carbonated beverages, inert atmospheres, and fire extinguishers for example.

To make a long story short, use *softgels* in oil form, CO_2 extraction at 320 mg a day and standardized 80 to 90 percent on EFA (essential fatty acid). Softgels are small, soft, smooth containers made from soft gelatin that are easy to swallow.

It is important for your saw palmetto to contain *Beta sitosterol,* which is very important for prostate health. Science has demonstrated that the most powerful supplement for prostate health is a common plant alcohol called Beta sitosterol. It is found in every vegetable. There are studies in France, Germany, Italy, Switzerland, Scotland, Pakistan, China, Brazil, the United States, and Belgium that confirm the importance of this plant alcohol. Beta sitosterol is found in saw palmetto, but watch it, most saw palmetto products sold in the United States have very little Beta sitosterol. Therefore, most products you find are useless. Even today, it is very difficult to find Beta sitosterol in drug stores, health food stores, and vitamin catalogs.

An additional positive effect of Beta sitosterol is that it can also reduce cholesterol.

So you need a saw palmetto product that contains Beta sitosterol. And you need a saw palmetto product that contains all its properties so that you get the effects you want to have.

Beta sitosterol from Soy

Now it is possible to extract Beta sitosterol from soy and get three thousand times more Beta sitosterol compared to the amount in saw palmetto. That does not mean it will work three thousand times better, but combined, both can work very well. One of the most important functions of Beta sitosterol is the reduction of the enzyme *5 Alpha reductas* (so less testosterone will convert into DHT.

Nettle Root Extract

Astonishing but true, it is a proven fact that nettle root extract can bind to prostate cells. There is an extract called *Urtica dicica* (often used in combination with saw palmetto) that can treat BPH.

Pygeum Africanum

Phyto is a Greek word meaning *simply plant.* Phytotherapeutics are simply therapeutical plant based methods, means, or mediums that can help in case of diseases. *Pygeum africanum* is phytotherapeutic. Pygeum africanum is a tree that grows in the high elevations of central and southern Africa. The bark is important. Africans used it for a long time for urinary problems. The bark contains substances with anti-inflammatory effects. It may reduce the risk of BPH and help improve urinary flow. Pygeum has the ability to reduce prostate swelling.

It may even help to prevent cancer. It definitely relieves the urinary symptoms, associated with BPH.

In other words, we have four powerful natural "weapons."

These four weapons (saw palmetto, beta -sitosterol from soy, stinging nettle, and pygeum africanum) are available today in standardized forms. Non-standardized versions of those plants exist as well, so we must beware. Additionally, some pharmaceutical companies do everything they can to substitute natural plant extracts (for patent reasons, for money). But we will skip all the problems encountered today with some drug companies, because we do no't want to write one hundred books. The good news is that natural sources cannot be legally "copyrighted." What is important for you is that you should look for excellent products that really have the effects you want.

Pumpkin Seed (Cucurbita pepo L.)

Besides those four major weapons, there are even more possibilities.

Let us quickly take a look.

After many studies in Europe, *pumpkin seed* is an approved drug in Germany for prostate enlargement. The fatty oil in pumpkin seeds is mildly diuretic, and the seeds' principal constituent, cucurbitacins, appears to inhibit the conversion of testosterone into dihydrotesterone. The presence of zinc and amino acids further help treat BPH.

Selenium is a potent antioxidant important in promoting and maintaining prostate health.

Pollen Flower works very well not only in prostatitis, but also in BPH (prostate enlargement).

L-Arginine

L-arginine is an *amino acid.* Amino acids occur naturally in plants and animals and are the basic constituents of *proteins.*

This amino acid (L-arginine) pumps up the body's natural supply of nitric oxide—an odorless gas made of nitrogen and oxygen that relaxes muscles and increases blood flow to vital organs, including the heart and penis. Quite frankly, if you don't have enough nitric oxide, your erection will be soft, limp, or, more likely, non existent.

L- Glycine and L- Glutamic Acid

Both L-arginine and L-glutamic acid are amino acids needed for maintaining normal prostate function.

L-glutamic acid is critical for proper cell function, but it is not considered an essential nutrient in humans because the body can manufacture it from simple compounds. In addition to being one of the building blocks in protein synthesis, it is also important in brain function.

Lignans from Flax Oil

Lignans are considered phytoestrogens. (Again, *phyto = plant; estrogen = a hormone*). By interacting with the complex mechanism of testosterone metabolism, lignans bring back the natural balance in hormone levels, reducing the effect of estradiol. A sufficient level of these lignans can compete with natural estrogen for the *estrogen receptors,* resulting in balanced *estrogen* levels in the blood.

Prostatitis and BPH are only two prostate problems. There is a third, more serious problem. Many people do not know that even with the more serious problems, natural healing options exist. However, before going on, let us summarize what we know so far.

Action

Information: Three main things can go wrong with the prostate: prostatitis (prostate infections), prostate enlargement (BPH), and prostate cancer.

Action: If a problem exists, see a doctor.

Information: There are four types of prostatitis: acute, bacterial, nonbacterial inflammation and an inflammation caused by muscle spasms.

Action: Today all four types of prostatitis can be managed; acute and chronic prostatitis with antibiotics, anti-inflammatories, immune boosters, and thermotherapy. And nonbacterial and muscle spasm -caused inflammation with hot baths, anti-inflammatory medication, and a change in diet. Also remember to avoid alcohol and coffee.

Information: Natural supplements that help with prostatitis: quercetin, pollen flower extract, borage oil, evening primrose oil, beta glucan, and IP6.

Action: In case of prostatitis, try natural supplements first.

Information: Benign prostatic hypertrophy (BPH) is found in one in six men between the ages of forty and fifty, one in four men fifty to sixty years old, one in two men sixty and above, and in men eighty and above, one in 1.2 men. The symptoms are: over dribbling urine flow, inability to empty the bladder completely, inability to urinate, difficulty holding urine, and interrupted sleep due to constant urination. BPH is classified into mild, moderate, and severe cases.

Action: If you have these symptoms, find out exactly what stage you are in.

Information: Possible tests for BPH are a digital rectal exam (DRE), urine test, and PSA (prostate specific antigen).

Action: Have the tests done and then get advice from your urologist. But always get a second opinion. Do not rush. Consider natural treatments first.

Information: Transurethral microwave thermotherapy (TUMT), transurethral needle ablation (TUNA), and high-intensity focused ultrasound (HIFU) are being used to treat BPH successfully.

Action: Try natural therapies first. If no success is achieved, look into TUMT, TUNA, and HIFU.

Information: There are a lot of natural treatments possible for patients with BPH. Do not jump into an operation too soon.

Action: First inform yourself as to what your possibilities are, and then decide what path to take.

Information: The most powerful natural substances for BPH are saw palmetto, Beta sitosterol, nettle root extract, pygeum africanum, pumpkin seed oil, pollen flower, L- arginine, L- glycine, glutamic acid, and lignans from flax.

Action: Watch for the quality of the product; they do not all have the same quality. Most saw palmetto products sold in the United States have no Beta sitosterol, for example.

VI

Prostate Cancer

Allow us to say something about cancer in general. Cancer is one of the most hated and feared words. Death, hopelessness, and apathy are connected to cancer. Some people think that it is too late for anything when they are diagnosed with cancer. Well, we differ. We think cancer has become a "no-word" that triggers the wrong associations. Cancer is in no way a death sentence. So we are against the emotional shock that accompanies this word.

A much more rational approach is necessary. We personally know many people who have had cancer, especially prostate cancer, that live fantastically good lives today. Just take a look at some celebrities and politicians who have had prostate cancer: Colin Powell, Bob Dole, Rudy Giuliani, General Norman Schwarzkopf, Jerry Lewis, and Sidney Poitier. John Kerry ran for the presidency of the United States just after a prostate cancer operation. The only real attitude that helps in relation to cancer is a non emotional attitude, a scientific approach.

We slowly grow into an age where we can fight cancer, discover its mechanisms, and develop more and more weapons to defeat it. Someday cancer will be utterly defeated, and there will come the time when we will laugh about cancer and the fear the word alone spreads. Many other once deadly diseases have now been eradicated. In the 1900s, the most common causes of death were influenza, diarrhea, dysentery, and tuberculosis. Not a problem today. In 1900, the life expectancy was forty years; today it is almost eighty. Those statistics speak for themselves, so let us attack the cancer rationale.

First, let us look at the word.

Hippocrates (460–370 front. J-C) made precise descriptions of cancer and used the Greek terms *carcinos* and *carcinoma* to indicate chronic ulcerations or sizes, which seemed to be malignant tumors.

According to the dictionary, *carcinos* means: crayfish, canker, or cancer (tumor).

Celsus (28 front. J-C.–50 ap. J-C), a Roman doctor, translated the Greek word carcinos into *cancer*. The Latin word means: (1) crab, crayfish, dunce and (2) cancer, canker. The term *cancer* indicated ulcers of malignant pace with major penetration. An assumption is that certain cancerous lesions evoked the shape of a crab; this explains the origin of the words *carcinos* and *cancer*. Galien (130–200) used the Greek term *oncos* to indicate a mass or a malignant tumor of pace. At the beginning of the nineteenth century, *carcinoma* became synonymous with *cancer*, and the termination *-oma* was used to refer to certain cancerous lesions.

The word *cancer* is thus very old. We see an analogy between the crab-to be precise, the claws of a crab–and cancer, which reach out and want to grab more. This was perhaps the reason the ancients called it cancer (crab). The cancer cells, when not under control, also reach out and want more. They grow.

There are many reasons and causes of cancer. There is a big genetic component, and a weak immune system plays a big role. Others contribute to the cause, such as viruses and special substances known as *carcinogens* that can trigger cancer. Think of all the polluted air, polluted water, chemicals in the food, in the kitchen, exposure to radioactivity, even heat and excessive sunlight, those are only some of the causes of cancer.

Cancer begins in cells, the body's basic unit of life. Cells have important functions throughout the body. Normally, cells grow and divide to form new cells in an ordered and controlled manner. They perform their functions for a while, and then they die. This process helps keep the body healthy. Sometimes, however, cells do not die. Instead, they keep dividing and creating new cells that the body does not need. They form a mass of tissue, called a tumor. Malignant tumors are cancer. Cells in these tumors are abnormal. They divide without control or order, and they do not die. They can invade and damage nearby tissues and organs. Also, cancer cells can break away from a malignant tumor and enter the bloodstream and lymphatic system. So cancer can spread from the original (primary) cancer site to form new (secondary) tumors in other organs. This spread of cancer is called *metastasis*. When prostate cancer spreads (metastasizes) outside the prostate, cancer cells are often found in nearby *lymph nodes*. If the cancer has reached these nodes, it means that cancer cells may have spread to other parts of the body—other lymph nodes and other organs, such as the bones, bladder, or rectum. When cancer spreads from its original locations to another part of the body, the new tumor has the same kind of abnormal cells and the same name as the primary tumor. For example, if prostate cancer spreads to the bones, the cancer cells in the new tumor are prostate cancer cells. The disease is *metastatic prostate cancer;* it is not *bone cancer.*

These are only facts. Now let us concentrate on the good news:

If you are diagnosed today with prostate cancer, your chances of recovery are excellent. Especially when the diagnosis is early enough. More good news is that prostate cancer is a primary cancer—as the doctors call it—which means that the condition starts in the prostate and does not automatically spread to other places in the body.

The best thing to do against cancer is to prevent it of course, but we will get back to that later. The second best thing to do is to detect cancer early enough so that it may be effectively treated. There is a far better chance of surviving if you detect cancer early. We can *do* something about cancer today.

But first some more facts about cancer:

- More than two hundred thirty-two thousand Americans are diagnosed with prostate cancer every year.
- This year, thirty thousand will die of the disease.
- One new case occurs every 2.5 minutes, and a man dies from prostate cancer every seventeen minutes.
- The top three types of newly diagnosed cancer in men:
  - Prostate cancer: 41 percent
  - Lung cancer: 13 percent (one hundred thousand newly diagnosed every year; the connection is smoking)
  - Colon and rectal cancer: 9 percent

Most prostate cancers are due to a combination of genetics (family history), and environmental factors (alcohol, diet, sunlight exposure).

Symptoms of localized prostate cancer are rare; warning signs do not usually appear until the cancer has escaped the prostate. Early detection is the key. In the end, more than two-thirds will survive this sort of cancer. Again, if you have a suspicion of cancer, the smartest thing you can do is to be certain. So tests are the talk of the day. What could you do?

Cancer Tests

The most common symptom of prostate cancer is no symptom at all.

Unfortunately, there is no positive symptom indicating cancer for sure.

By the time symptoms occur, the disease may have spread beyond the prostate. When symptoms do occur, they may include:

- Frequent urination, especially at night
- Inability to urinate
- Trouble starting or holding back urination
- A weak or interrupted flow of urine
- Painful or burning urination
- Blood in the urine or semen
- Painful ejaculation
- Frequent pain in the lower back, hips, or upper thighs

These can be symptoms of cancer, but, more often, they are symptoms of non-cancerous conditions. It is very important to check with a doctor. There exists a variety of cancer tests. The most popular is still the *digital rectal examination*. The *digit* is the urologist's probing finger. This finger is introduced into the rectum, and the doctor tries to feel for ridges, nodes, hard spots, etc. Also a genital inspection usually follows. The external genitals are checked, the shape of the penis, the scrotum. Sometimes cancer can be detected this way. If there is suspicion of cancer, other tests follow, such as the PSA-test and the free PSA test or PSA II. PSA stands for prostate specific antigen.

This is a blood test, showing the amount for *antigens* in the prostate. What is an antigen? *Anti* means *against,* and *gen* means *genus* or *kind.* Antigen is a protein substance in humans and animals that helps to create antibodies. But we do not even have to know that. We only have to know that those antigens have a special *level,* and they are only found in the prostate. If this protein substance level is above normal, then cancer probably exists.

Not all PSA tests are the same. In fact, there are more than thirty tests in use today in Europe, and six in the U.S. The results may vary from test to test, so it is important not to change the type of test. The annual PSA test should be done with the same laboratory each time, and the same brand of test should be used. This test, a blood test, has the advantage that nearly no pain is present. Unnecessary prostate biopsies can be avoided.

Actually, about 70 percent of all men do not have any symptoms of cancer when they are diagnosed with prostate cancer.

Free PSA or PSA II

Free PSA is the percentage of the total PSA that circulates in the blood without a carrier protein. The lower the percentage, the more likely it is to get prostate cancer. Those who have it below 20 percent probably have cancer. Free PSA may eventually allow us to forego biopsy altogether in men with PSA between four and ten and a free PSA of >24.

Values suggestive of prostate cancer:

Total PSA 3.9 to four with a free PSA of < 19 percent.

Total PSA four to ten with a free PSA of < 17 to 24 percent.

PSA doubling time (PSADT) is the time it takes for the PSA value to double. This may be useful in following up on treatment and determining the type of treatment.

PSA velocity (PSAV) refers to the rate of change in PSA levels over time. It is the rate of change of PSA calculated per year. The normal PSAV is 0. That means no change in a year. PSA levels normally should not change in ten years. If the PSA is starting to rise, something is wrong and you must act. The faster the PSAV, the shorter the PSADT.

For example, if last year your PSA level was two, and now it is four. The PSADT (the time to double the PSA) is one year. The PSAV is two in a year, a change from two to four. In this case, you probably have cancer and need further testing. It is very important to keep your PSA results over the years, so you can calculate the PSAV and PSADT.

Chart 2: Effects on ejaculation on PSA levels.

Ejaculation increases the serum prostate-specific antigen

concentration.

According to a study done at the Michigan Prostate Institute, University of Michigan, published in The Journal of Urology in 1996, conducted with sixty-four men aged forty-nine to seventy-nine years, who underwent a serum PSA determination immediately before ejaculation (baseline) and at one hour, six hours, and twenty-four hours following ejaculation. The serum PSA also was measured at forty-eight hours and one week after ejaculation if the concentration had not returned to the baseline value by the previous time interval.

More Tests

There are more tests. *Prostatic acid phosphatase* (PAP) is a blood test that is usually done after a tissue biopsy. It shows if the cancer has spread to other regions of the body. In the *ultrasound,* sound waves are projected against the prostate, they echo from the prostate and are converted into an image. *Computerized axial topography* (CT scan) describes a whole series of photographs done with the X-ray technique. A computer puts those photographs together into a three-dimensional image. *Magnetic resonance imaging* (MRI) uses magnetic techniques to get a picture of the prostate. In the end, biopsies are still the only sure way to know if there is cancer present or not. A thin needle is put into the body, through the rectum or the skin near the anal opening. Some samples are taken and looked at under the microscope.

Horrible? Of course it is horrible. Who wants it? But all those examinations may be necessary. Remember, the earlier it is detected, the less powerful the cancer is. Most people assume, by the way, that prostate cancer grows in a single spot within the gland. Not true. Average prostate cancer starts in seven different malignant spots; an urologist can check those spots.

Grading System

So let us assume the worst-case scenario: cancer. Again, even if you are diagnosed with cancer, you should not panic. Why? You can do a lot! The next step consists of determining what *grade* of cancer it is. So determining the exact stage of cancer is really important, because most cancers are treatable today.

There are additional tests that can show how far the cancer has spread.

We already mentioned CT (computer axial topography) scan and MRI (magnetic resonance imaging) scan, but also chest X-rays can be used or *bone scans* which can find advanced prostate cancer (metastasis).

Again, you need to determine exactly how aggressive, how bad, the cancer really is. The grading technique used in most cases is the *Gleason grading system*. Here, the two most representative areas of the tumor will be examined under a microscope. Then the pathologist assigns a grade between one and five to those two representative areas. Grade one means the cancer is not very dangerous and will probably not spread. Grade five means the cancer will probably grow fast. Then the pathologist adds those two grades and gives an overall evaluation of the cancer between two and ten. The scores are as follows: two to four—cancer growing slowly, and six to ten-cancer is very aggressive. There are other grading tests, like the *Mostofi grading system* that uses Roman numerals. Grade I is comparable to a two to four on the Gleason test, but in both tests, cancers are assigned a stage. The *Whitmore-Jewett Test* or *ABCD staging system* assigns letters to cancer from A-to D. An A or B means the cancer is only in the prostate region. A C or D means the cancer has spread beyond the prostate or throughout the body. Another system is called the *TNM staging system*. T stands for tumor, N for nodes, and M for metastasis. M, of course, means the cancer has spread; T is the size of the tumor, and N is whether it has reached the lymph nodes. However, the crucial point always is has cancer spread into the rest of the body or not? If not, there is a good chance it can be handled.

Attacking the Attacker

Whatever stage of cancer a person is in; there are methods to deal with it. Let us look at the most common ones before we give the alternative that gives hope. Never forget that: scientists are searching like mad to find better ways to detect and treat cancer. It is no overstatement to say that we are getting better every day.

However, how is cancer *usually* treated today? Prostate cancer *surgery* is still No. 1. With a scalpel or a laser, the cancerous tissue is removed, eliminated. The problem is that sometimes the cancer comes back. Also side effects are common, including incontinence and impotence.

Radiation therapy is another way. With high-energy particles, the prostate cancer cells get bombarded. A newer technique consists of tiny capsules containing a radioactive substance that are implanted into the prostate tumor through surgery. The advantage is that the whole prostate in not under assault. These capsules are supposed to kill the cancer, too.

Drug treatment is again another way of treating cancer. Unfortunately, there has never been a wonder pill against cancer, but rather many pills with frightening side effects. Actually, we do not like to talk about drugs, because drugs usually have so many side effects that they are difficult to count.

Hormonal therapy is another way. The conventional hormone therapy for prostate cancer is to reduce testosterone levels to 0. We do not like that either. Why? As we wrote at the beginning of the book, free testosterone will do much more good than bad for your body. You can reduce estrogen (estradiol) and DHT and improve free testosterone and progesterone, and that way balance your hormones. You don't need to feel castrated. By the way, the results with this treatment are not good in the long term. At the beginning, you can see PSA drop to 0, but, in two to four years, it will start increasing again.

We believe men have other natural treatments that can help them avoid feeling castrated, but let us continue:

Chemotherapy is usually not used in treating prostate cancer. The results are very poor.

Hyperthermia tries to bombard the cancer with high levels of heat.

Cryosurgery is another alternative. *Cryos* means *frost* and is the root word of cryosurgery. For some people, *cryosurgery* appears to be more effective than current standard treatments. This freezing treatment is sometimes offered as an alternative treatment, and, yes, it is less invasive, and seems to bring about fewer complications. Nevertheless, it is not without risk.

Angiogenesis inhibitors are another alternative. *Angio* means blood vessels, *genesis* means formation. So *angiogenesis* = the growth and proliferation of blood vessels. To develop and metastasize, cancer cells need blood vessels around the tumor. If we can stop the blood vessel growth, we can stop the tumor from growing and spreading. There are many clinical trials running now in different parts of the country with several different drugs that may have an anti-angiogenesis effect. For example, *thalidomide,* used in the '60s to reduce nausea in pregnant women, is being tested. Unfortunately, as a side effect, thousands of babies were born without arms and legs. That happened because the drug had an anti-angiogenesis effect. Now it is being used in cancer. In addition, *shark cartilage* substances are being studied to unravel their anti-angiogenesis properties. Some natural plants may also have a similar effect, such as an extract from *convolvulus arvensis,* for example.

These are roughly spoken, traditional treatments when it comes to cancer. How should you evaluate them? Well, go to a surgical-oriented urologist, and he will praise and glorify his method. Go to a chemotherapist, and he will tell you his method is the best. Go to a third specialist, and he will tell you that his method is the only one. Every method has its risks, and it is impossible to make a general statement for each and every cancer patient. But we dare make three statements:

1. Inform yourself first. Do not allow anyone to talk you into a therapy you don't believe in and/or you know nothing about. There is a lot of information out there about each therapy. Learn.
2. Usually surgery prolongs life, yes, but the disadvantages are the loss of natural sexual function (most common) and the loss of normal urination (least common).

    Plus, there is never a guarantee that the cancer will not come back, and there are many possible side effects.
3. You can't go wrong when you take a look at the natural treatments, which usually can improve your health condition, even cancer. Watchful waiting may be correct sometimes with the advice to regularly check your prostate to see if cancer grows there or not. In fact, changing lifestyles can sometimes prevent an operation. Additionally, there are supplements in existence today that really do something to the prostate. They are natural supplements, that can even *heal* the prostate in a significant amount of cases.

With all the information we have given you, you can easily see that "health" is not the absence of disease, nor is it not an absolute state. "Health," metaphorically, is "white" in a range where black is disease, a cancer spreading all over your body. We live within that range of grays. "Health" is not an absolute;

"disease" is not an absolute.

Your body is usually within one of those different grays, and, in fact, we could define one hundred different shades of gray, not only A, B, C, or D. This means that you can go back from black to a deep gray to a light gray or perhaps even to white. Illness is a process, that may take many years to establish. Health could be considered to be similar. You can go back to a healthy state, a healthy body environment, if you know some rules, some laws, and some supplements. The most exciting discoveries have been made when it comes to "going back to health," especially when it is related to the prostate. Also never forget, the smartest way to deal with cancer is not getting it in the first place. There are ways to avoid cancer and heal the early stages of cancer in a natural way. So let's summarize our knowledge, and then, without further delay, let's get right to it.

Action

Information: The earlier the detection of prostate cancer, the better the chances. Two -thirds of the people diagnosed with prostate cancer survive.

Action: If there is the suspicion of prostate cancer, get tested fast.

Get a complete physical (including a digital rectal exam) every year after you turn forty.

Information: Cancer is due to a combination of genetics and environment.

Action: Avoid alcohol, bad diet, and too much sunlight.

Information: There are many tests you can take:
- Digital rectal examination
- PSA
- Free PSA or PSA II
- PSADT
- PSAV
- Prostatic acid phosphatase (PAP), a blood test
- Ultrasound
- Computerized axial topography (CT) scan
- Magnetic resonance imaging (MRI)
- Biopsy

Action: Do the necessary tests.

Information: There are several grading systems in evaluating cancer:

- Gleason's grading system (Grade 1, not very dangerous; Grade 5, cancer growing fast).
- Whitmore-Jewett-Test (ABCD staging system)
- TNM staging system (T = tumor, N = nodes, M = metastasis)

Action: If you do have prostate cancer, find out exactly which stage it is in.

Information: There are many possible treatments for prostate cancer: surgery, radiation therapy, drug treatment, hormonal therapy, chemotherapy, hypothermia, and cryosurgery.

Action: Before deciding, inform yourself. Do not jump into a treatment if you are not totally convinced by it. There are dangers and side effects associated to all of these treatments.

VII.

Prostate Cancer and Nutrition

It may very well be that the art of nutrition will be the key to healthy aging. What we know already about the relationship between eating and health, and even between eating and cancer, is nothing short of astonishing. Just consider this: men in the Far East, in China and Japan, have usually 90 percent less prostate cancer than men in the United States. That's 90 percent. This is a fact, it is not wishful thinking, it is not guessing. Scientists concluded that men in those countries must do something right. A group of researchers, doctors, scientists, statisticians, and urologists therefore started to look deeper into this subject. First, they guessed that this fact must have something to do with the genes. But many scientists had already over-estimated the power of genes. The genes were once the talk of the day, they were responsible for everything, but scientists learned that genes are important, but by far not as important as originally envisioned. However, investigators and inquirers actually found out that genes are not the reason why men in the United States have prostate cancer. So they carefully researched the rate of prostate cancer in Japanese men who moved to the United States from Japan. Guess what they found? Yes, Japanese men developed even more prostate cancer than American men. These migration studies were repeated, all with the same result. The moment Japanese or Chinese people moved away from their home countries, prostate cancer inevitably increased.

Of course, the attention immediately turned to the diet. The Western diet was compared to the Eastern diet. The differences were evident. Americans eat hamburgers, cheeseburgers, potatoes, French fries, and pizza; while in the Far East, men eat soy products, rice, and vegetables. In short, it was a totally different diet.

More studies were done. Additionally, the Western diet is, to a great extent, heavily polluted and industrialized. And the diet is based mainly on animal products, meat, and dairy products and is higher in fat. By far, less vegetables and fruits are eaten in the U.S. and lots of sugar and starch products instead. Some people did not like the findings, but the facts were clear: in China, only two persons out of one hundred thousand people develop prostate cancer. Cancer is practically not an issue in China. In the United States, the cancer rate is thirty-six times higher. Again, the conclusion was obvious.

The attention of the scientific world turned to the diet. Here, a war was nearly started over the discussion of which diet is the "right" one. Diets are different everywhere. Look at the number of books about the "right" diet that are published in the U.S. every year.

Nevertheless the picture got clearer and clearer.

It couldn't be ignored any longer; the devils in the prostate cancer war were:

- Animal fats
- Preserved foods
- Preserved meats
- Preserved vegetables
- Not enough vegetables
- Not enough fruits
- Clinically treated food
- Unusual amounts of sugar in all forms
- An unusual amount of starches, such as pizzas and

white, refined flour.

The traditional Chinese diet, on the other hand, contained:

- Lots of garlic, scallions, and onions
- Fiber
- Plenty of fruits
- Lots of soybeans
- Lots of vegetables, especially green vegetables.

So it is not surprising that the American Cancer Society tells us to return to the diet we ate when we were evolving, more vegetables, more fruit, less barbecue, and more aerobic exercise are needed.

Wrong diets are the major cause of prostate cancer. So "prostate cancer diets" were designed in the following years to protect against prostate cancer. Again research, research, and more research were undertaken. The result was astonishing: even patients already diagnosed with prostate cancer could alter the course of their disease just with a change in diet.! New words were created, such as nutritional therapies, and chemoprevention, and the sun was shining again.

Today about 30 percent of prostate cancer patients use prostate cancer diets with great results. Of course, scientists looked deep into different diets to find out the exact food, the exact ingredient that could prevent cancers from growing. And, again, scientists struck pure gold. But before taking this up, let us first clear up some basics so that we know what we are talking about.

The Basics

You should know that hardly any subject is as confusing as the subject of nutrition. Nutrition is big money, and one should be aware of that. Every nutrition- producer, every nutrition company, can hire a few scientists and make them say what they would like to hear. "Science" is seldom neutral and objective, despite what we all would like to believe. You can even find advertising promoting candies, saying that candies are good for energy and that they help the body. Nothing could be farther away from the truth, and you must know this.

These false "authorities" trick us into misusing words. Words can be redefined, twisted, used in wrong context, and new words can be invented, twisted again, and given a second or a third meaning there is a whole science of how to lie efficiently. Usually the money is the motivator behind all of those efforts. Big industries make hundreds of billions of dollars every year selling unhealthy, life-threatening nutrition and doing everything to make sure that the truth does not spread.

A way of defeating all those efforts is clearing up words. If you know the definition of a word, you can judge things by yourself and nobody can twist your opinion. Therefore, a good dictionary is more important than a good car.

However, there are some basics concepts you must know if you are interested in judging for yourself and making up your own mind. So let us take a close look at what nutrition is all about.

Basically, you have to differentiate between *proteins, fats,* and *carbohydrates.* Proteins, simply put, are mainly found in meat, poultry eggs, fish, beens etc. The word *protein* stems from the Greek word *protos,* which means first. So the first thing we need is protein, excluding water, which, of course, is even more important. You can get protein from some plants as well. Along with protein, we need to take in a lot of vitamins, B1, B2, B6, and B12, and also zinc.

So what is the problem with protein? We are exposed to antibiotics and hormones in the usual meat we eat. To make a long story short, about 90 percent of the meat available today on the market is low quality meat. So nothing is wrong with the meat itself, it is the quality of the meat that is wrong.

Now we come to a wonderful and misleading word: *carbohydrates*. The word infers that it is food made out of *carbon* and *hydrogen*. (*Oxygen* is part of it, too). All sugars and starches are *carbohydrates*. Cakes, candies, pastas, pizzas, potatoes-these are all carbohydrates. Billions of wrong misleading advertisements are put out every year promoting carbohydrates. The results can be seen everywhere: people get sick and fat.

Companies get away with misleading advertising because there are *good carbohydrates* as well. Wait a minute. What are "good carbohydrates?" Good carbohydrates are green vegetables, for example. They also are called *complex carbohydrates*. "Bad carbohydrates" are bad because they are refined and lack nutrients, such as vitamins and fiber, for example. In other words, the first thing one has to understand is that there is a huge difference between *refined* carbohydrates and *complex* carbohydrates.

So there are "good carbohydrates" and "bad carbohydrates." Green lettuce = good. Rice cakes with sugar = bad. Of course, there are lots of degrees between good and bad carbohydrates.

Now what about fats? That we all need fat is a well-established fact in scientific knowledge. Fats are needed in every cell. Fats can come from animal sources (eggs, chicken, beef, etc.), and they can be derived from plant sources (avocados, olives, nuts, and seeds.). What is the best fat? Well, organic cold-pressed olive oil and organic cold-pressed flax oil, for example. Of course, one could get far more sophisticated than that. But at least we now have some idea about proteins, carbohydrates, and fats.

Now back to our subject: prostate cancer and nutrition.

Scientists worked day and night to find out what ingredients work best to stop prostate cancer from growing and to hinder prostate cancer from developing at all. Their findings are worth pure gold.

Prostate Cancer-Killers

Here is the first surprise: scientific findings state that when it comes to protein, the best source of protein (in relation to prostate cancer) is soy protein. The reasons are that some components of soy restrict blood vessel growth and inhibit certain enzymes. In addition, there is a substance found in soy roots called *genistein*. Technically speaking, genistein is a plant estrogen. "But estrogen is bad," you say, if you really read this book carefully. Yes, but *genistein* only has one-thousandth of the power of full-strength estrogen. So, genistein is a plant estrogen, and it acts like an anti-cancer agent. Cancer needs blood vessels to develop, to spread, and to metastasize. Genistein seems to prevent just that. The signal to increase cell growth, cancer cell growth, seems to be stopped by genistein from soy. Therefore, when it comes to nutrition, soy is the first soldier in our fight for prostate health.

No Insulin

Another dietary factor found to be of extreme importance to avoid prostate cancer is insulin. Insulin promotes the growth factor in prostate cells. Elevated insulin occurs with elevated levels of blood fats and blood sugar called glucose. But how can you avoid high insulin levels? High insulin is caused by excess starch (bad carbohydrates), sugar, and fat. Low insulin is achieved by eating fruits, fiber, and vegetables. So cut out sugars, bad carbohydrates, and refined flours. Eat beans, vegetables, and fruits, and get organic products. In addition, high-fiber foods and those containing whole grain help with prostate cancer. But what foods contain fiber?

Fiber

The *fiber* factor has been forgotten in the Western diet. Many studies demonstrate, beyond doubt, the advantages of fiber in the prevention of heart diseases, diabetes, obesity, and cancer, including prostate cancer.

So go for *soluble fiber,* which you find in vegetables, such as brussels sprouts, most beans, and soybeans, some fruits, such as apples, and also in oats, rice, and whole grains. With these, the prostate problems can be attacked in a natural way. So you can *do* something about it. The truth is the good news does not end here. There is even more that we can do in fighting prostate cancer.

Vitamins

Nearly a century ago, the role of vitamin was detected. In 1912, Dr. Erik Fink, a Norwegian biochemist, isolated the first vitamin. English biochemist I. G. Hopkins continued the research. In 1913, McCollum and Davis, two American researchers, discovered a substance called vitamin A. In the months and years after that, more and more vitamins were discovered. McCollum and Davis discovered vitamin B, followed by vitamins C, D, and E, and so it went through the alphabet. The world was stunned. Vitamin A could help with bad eyesight, B1 could cure infections, B6 was great for muscle problems, and vitamin C was good for one hundred other maladies and was almost the universal problem solver. Nutrition entered a new age. The possibilities seemed fantastic. In Japan, in the United States, in Germany, and many other European countries, vitamins became something people talked about enthusiastically. *Vita,* Latin for *life,* seemed to be newly discovered, and, in fact, many a break-through has been made possible thanks to vitamins. Vitamins, in the correct dosage, are "natural" and have no side effects, as do drugs. Researchers found, without a doubt, that vitamins help when it comes to prostate cancer. But you must know that today vitamins are a science in itself. There are different qualities of vitamins. You should use only natural vitamins rather than synthetic ones. Additionally, vitamins must be balanced out with each other. Nevertheless, vitamins are a great source for health.

Now which is important for prostate cancer? Vitamin D. Why? Scientists established an interesting fact: the farther north a person lives, the higher the risk of prostate cancer. The reason is because in the north there is less ultraviolet light available. In Scandinavian countries (Finland, Sweden, Norwegian) and in North America, especially Canada, the ultraviolet light is low. Ultraviolet light is necessary for the manufacturing of vitamin D. The sun's rays, ultraviolet sunrays, stimulate the creation of vitamin D in the body. Dark-skinned people have a serious problem: the color of their skin absorbs *less* ultraviolet light. So who is at a greater risk of prostate cancer? Men with dark skin living in northern climates.

However, vitamin D is of special importance for the prostate. Scientific studies show that the growth of prostate cancer cells slow down when vitamin D attaches to the cancer cells. Vitamin D also helps in the case of BPH. Vitamin D acts as a brake in a car driving toward prostate cancer. Two hundred to 400 international units per day seem to be optimal. A special form of vitamin D, called 1, 25 dihydroxyvitamin D (nickname: 1, 25 D), discovered by Dr. David Feldman M.D., is the best sort of vitamin D to help with prostate cancer. One, 25 D works best as an antigrowth agent. So you could take this, but, in addition, you should also get sunlight or, rather, should seek sunlight. The fact is: solar radiation may provide 75 percent of the necessary vitamin D. However, excess sunlight may promote skin- cancer. There is a simple solution: just fifteen minutes three times a week or ten minutes every day in the sunlight is enough. So you don't need that much sunlight. By the way, the sun is best in the morning, until 10 AM, and very good after 4 PM. The sun during the hottest time (noon) should be avoided.

Exercise

The advantageous effects of exercise on health have long been established. There is no doubt that exercise has many benefits. Literally hundreds, perhaps thousands, of studies have been undertaken to prove the positive effects of exercise. The human body has to be moved. Without movement and use, it gets old and stops working properly, comparable to the motor of a vehicle, which also has to be used to operate optimally. Exercise has positive effects on longevity, the heart, and the immune system. But here is the kicker: Dr. Ralph Paffenbarger has established that men over seventy who maintain high levels of exercise are 50 percent less likely to get prostate cancer. Nothing could be more stunning. So there is no question that you should exercise regularly if you have prostate cancer or wants to prevent it. The question is: What exercise? How much? How often? How intense? Well, the key is to build an exercise routine bit by bit, starting low, and progressing to higher levels. There is nothing more foolish than jumping into an extreme exercise program from Day One. Additionally, the type of exercise has to be established individually. Doctors' recommendations include walking, running, swimming, or biking, but there are hundreds of other possible exercises from aerobics to football and tennis. From a health standpoint, the best exercises are walking, running, swimming, and biking. Many books have been written about each one of those exercises and many others. You should be professional, learn about the specific exercise first, and then start. It is said that exercising only two times a week for one hour maintains your health level. But exercising everyday improves your health. So exercising daily is better than only one or two days a week.

Back to our subject. Many prostate programs exist where exercise plays a part. Many other positive effects of exercise can be expected, such as an improvement in the mood, an increase of antioxidant defense, and the betterment of immune functions. The best exercise is, of course, an exercise that you really like. And maximum impact on the maximum amount of muscles is better than exercises that train just one part of the body. The rise of workout stations may be a great help in exercising, especially when one can find a professional who shows how to exercise the best. But watch it, extreme exercise, like a marathon everyday, is definitely not good. Too much stress on the bones, joints, and muscles will have a negative effect. Altogether, the best exercises seem to be running, outside, in nature, where you have fresh air and sunlight at the same time. Outdoors is better than indoors, but exercising indoors with a view you enjoy will do the job, too.

Stress

Stress is felt when demands are not met. When a job is too stressful, it means that it is difficult to meet the expectations of the job. A relationship is stressful when one or both of the spouses are not satisfied. You feel stressed when you are unhappy.

The least understood factor today is the word *stress* since it seems to embrace everything: professional relationships, work atmosphere, relationships with friends and partners, and even more, the relationship with the environment. We know today that little activity is bad, and an environment with no challenge at all is not positive. On the other hand, too much stress can definitely lead to maladies and illnesses. There is probably not an objective standard for stress: some people can take a lot of stress, both physical stress and psychological stress. The individual stress level can also be very low. Think about the amount of stress a person who is running for the American presidency has lsuch as John Kerry who just had a prostate operation. Imagine the overwhelming stress everyday. Enduring attacks, slander, hits, suppressions, oppressions, and lies. Most people could not stand a single day of such a life.

So stress is very individualized, and one must find his own optimum stress level. Without a doubt, a good stable relationship with a partner is of extreme importance, and, needless to say, sex should be optimal for both. Experts advise normal activity in relation to sex, not too little and not too much.

Aristotle, the philosopher of the "golden midst," seems to be right two thousand years later. A partnership or marriage with stress, quarrels, troubles, and misunderstandings pervaded by negativity is, of course, counter productive. This can be reflected in prostate cancer or prostate problems. If your love life is not good, do something about it. Things will not change miraculously, but work with your spouse on making each other happy. Listen to each other's needs and compromise. If you cannot do it on your own, seek counseling. Choose your friends. Ban negative people from your life, people who create problems, and cause stress. Seek good people, people you can trust. Avoid dealing with people who stress you out. There is no contract with God, saying you have to be oppressed all the time. However, the connection between stress and cancer has been well established through scientific studies. Statistically, high amounts of stress lead to prostate cancer. Why? It is an interesting question, even exciting. Above all body functions, all body laws, there seem to be *affect*. It is what you feel deep inside, and what affects the way your mind operates. Positive emotions (feeling loved and accepted) actually trigger the production of opiates (dopamine, serotonin) that give you a feeling of well- being. Furthermore, emotions modulate the production of cortisol, which sends you into a state of alert phylogenetically designed to fend from physical danger, as when your body is prepared to flee. That is why people who are stressed refer to being so tired physically.

As we know today, affect even monitors the hormones. If your emotions are full of stress, if you constantly have "black thoughts," so to say, it can throw your hormones out of balance. Hormones again are responsible for a lot of body functions, as we already know even optimum blood. But white blood cells cannot fight at optimal levels when there are black thoughts, bad thoughts, and negative thoughts. Also the nervous system obeys the hormone system, but, again, the hormone system obeys the emotions. Even your immune system is put on hold when under stress; therefore, over time, unhappiness weakens the immune system. There are even immune suppressant hormones, such as the famous cortisol. But let's stay with the simple truth: stress weakens the immune system, and a weakened immune system cannot fight cancer. Marital conflicts, an oppressive boss, and problem-creating people can all switch off the immune system and, in turn, diminish the fight against cancer. It is as simple as that.

It is neither a matter of denying our problems nor avoiding them. It does not help just to think positively since this causes more stress to our mind: being in denial requires a lot of energy. It is a matter of appraising our situation and solving it.

This is even true with simple colds. When there is little or no stress, a cold is not as tough as when there is a lot of stress. So, yes, stress can be linked to cancer, without a doubt. Depression, distress, bad feelings, bad thoughts can all affect one's health. Wise men have always said, laughter is the best medicine, and they were right.

So take the necessary steps not to be stressed. At work, when tired or stressed take a break, turn off the light, and take a ten-minute walk. At home, solve the issues that prevent you from having a satisfying relationship. Avoid chronic stress and even acute stress by solving your problems and by seeking regular relaxation. This is an additional way to fight prostate cancer.

So one can do a lot about prostate cancer these days. Prostatitis and BPH are things that can be handled, and even the word prostate cancer has lost a lot of its shock- effect. Today there are many weapons in existence to fight cancer. Again, the statistics say that two-thirds of the people with prostate cancer will survive. Applying *all* of the possible techniques available will increase this percentage remarkably. But there is even more one can do directly.

Key Tools to Fight Prostate Cancer

There are four key tools you can apply to fight prostate cancer directly.

These key tools are:

1. Balance hormone levels (You need normal levels of free testosterone, low levels of estrogen (estradiol), and low levels of DHT. Good levels of progesterone, DHEA, and pregnenolone are also part of the picture.
2. Take antioxidants and natural cancer fighters
3. Use immune system boosters
4. Use angiogenesis inhibitors

Natural Supplements to Complete Each Task

Allow us to give you the following information. You don't have to clear up each word immediately; we will look at some much closer later.

1. To balance your hormone levels:
    - Testosterone cream
    - Androstenedione
    - Progesterone
    - DHEA
    - Pregnenolone
    - Beta sitosterol
    - Zinc
    - Lignans
    - Nettle root

- Saw palmetto
- Pygeum africanum
- Pumpkin seed oil
- Chrysin
- DIM
- Eurycoma longifolia jack
- Tribulus terrestris
- Maca-lepidium meyenii G
- Muira puama

2. Antioxidants:
   - Selenium
   - Vitamin E
   - Lycopene
   - EFA, GLA, flax oil
   - Resveratrol
   - Green tea
   - Isoflavones

3. Immune system boosters:
   - Beta glucan
   - IP6
   - Ellagic acid
   - AHCC
   - Maitake D Fraction
   - Colostrum
   - MGN3

4. Angiogenesis inhibitors:
   - Convolvulus arvensis
   - Shark Cartilage

Now let us look at some of those words more exactly, and the scientific findings that go together with them.

Selenium and Vitamin E

The Selenium and Vitamin E Cancer Prevention Trial (SELECT) is a research study to determine if selenium and vitamin E can help prevent prostate cancer. SELECT is funded by the National Cancer Institute and coordinated by the Southwest Oncology Group. More than four hundred study sites in the U.S., Canada, and Puerto Rico are enrolling men in SELECT. Approximately thirty-two thousand men from the United States, Puerto Rico, and Canada will participate in the study. SELECT is the largest-ever prostate cancer prevention trial. Previous studies suggest that selenium and vitamin E (alone or in combination) may reduce the risk of developing prostate cancer by 30 to 60 percent, but only a large clinical trial such as SELECT can confirm those initial findings. SELECT began enrolling patients on August 22, 2001, and hopes to enroll 32,400 men over a five-year period. As of August 2003, SELECT had enrolled 24,639 men, or 76 percent of the targeted goal. The trial has now entered its third year of enrollment.

Lycopene

Lycopene, a carotenoid without pro-vitamin-A activity, is present in many fruits and vegetables. It is a red, fat-soluble pigment found in certain plants and microorganisms, including tomatoes and tomato-based products. Lycopene is also found in watermelon, papaya, pink grapefruit, and pink guava. It is more bioavailable (better aborbed and ready to be used in our body) in both processed and cooked tomato products than from fresh tomatoes. Dietary intake of tomatoes and tomato products containing lycopene have shown to be associated with a decreased risk of chronic diseases, such as cancer and cardiovascular disease, in cell culture, animal, and epidemiological investigations. In addition, serum and tissue *lycopene* levels have been inversely correlated with risk of lung and prostate cancers. Many studies suggest that lycopene may reduce the risk of prostate cancer.

Isoflavones

Isoflavones are a subclass of flavonoids. In contrast to the flavonoids, isoflavones have a more limited distribution in nature. Isoflavones that can be found in soybeans include glycine, daidzein, glycetin, and genistein. These compounds are known antioxidants, and genistein has been shown to influence signal transduction through its effect on several enzymes. Isoflavones may have positive effects on humans, such as cancer inhibition, increased bone strength, and a decrease in heart disease.

Green Tea

Green tea is rich in the flavonol group of polyphenols known as catechins. The fermentation process used in making black tea destroys the biologically active polyphenols of the fresh leaf. The catechins as a group have significant free radical scavenging ability and are potent antioxidants. Four catechins are found in green tea leaves:

Epicatechin (EC)
Epigallocatechin (EGC)
Epicatechin gallate (ECG)
Epigallocatechin gallate (EGCG)

Of these four factions, EGCG is the most important to the prostate cancer patient. Pharmacological activity extends beyond its actions as an antioxidant and free radical scavenger. Epigallocatechin-3 gallate (EGCG) acts against urokinase, an enzyme often found in large amounts in human cancers (Jankun et al., *Nature*, 1997). Urokinase breaks down the basement membrane of cell junctions, which may be a key step in the process of tumor cell metastasis, as well as tumor growth (Ennis et al., *Proc. Annu. Meet. Am. Assoc. Cancer Res.*, 1997).

EGCG attaches to urokinase and prevents these actions.

Long-term consumption of tea catechins is common in China and Japan. The frequency of the latent, localized type of prostate cancer does not vary significantly between Eastern and Western cultures, but the clinical incidence of metastatic prostate cancer is generally lower in Japan and other Asian countries, in contrast to the common occurrence of metastatic prostate cancer in Europe and the United States. One possible explanation is that EGCG consumption in green tea in Asian countries prevents the progression and metastasis of prostate cancer cells. This explains the lower mortality rate due to prostate and breast cancer in Asian countries as compared to Western countries.

Again, prostate cancer is one of the common cancers among men, in the U.S. At least a quarter of all prostate cancer patients use alternative therapies, including green tea. Some researchers noted that recent animal epidemiological studies suggest that green tea may have anti-tumor effects against carcinoma of the prostate.

EFA (Essential Fatty Acid): Marine Fish Oil

Experimental studies suggest that marine fatty acids have an antitumor effect on prostate tumor cells. The aim of this study was to investigate whether high consumption of fish and marine fatty acids reduces the risk of prostate cancer in humans. We followed 47,882 men participating in the Health Professionals Follow-up Study. Dietary intake was assessed in 1986, 1990, and 1994, using a validated food frequency questionnaire. During twelve years of follow-up, 2,482 cases of prostate cancer were diagnosed, of which six hundred seventeen were diagnosed as advanced prostate cancer, including two hundred seventy-eight metastatic prostate cancers. Eating fish more than three times per week was associated with a reduced risk of prostate cancer, and the strongest association was for metastatic cancer.

Prostate cancer risk and consumption of fish oils: a dietary biomarker-based case-control study.

—*Norrish, A. E., Skeaff, C. M., Arribas, G. L., Sharpe, S. J., Jackson. R. T., Department of Community Health, University of Auckland, New Zealand.*

The authors examined the relationship between prostate cancer risk and EPA (eicosa-apentaenoic acid)and DHA (docosapentaenoic acid) in erythrocyte biomarkers in a population-based case-control study in Auckland, New Zealand during 1996-1997, involving three hundred seventeen prostate cancer cases and four hundred eighty age-matched community controls. Reduced prostate cancer risk was associated with high erythrocyte phosphatidylcholine levels of EPA.

These analyses support evidence from in vitro experiments for a reduced risk of prostate cancer associated with dietary fish oils, possibly acting via inhibition of arachidonic acid-derived eicosanoid biosynthesis.

Essential fatty acids-contained in large amounts of fatty fish, for example-have been proven to inhibit the growth of prostate cancer cells. Paul Terry and colleagues from the Karolinska Institute, Stockholm, Sweden, followed more than six thousand Swedish men age fifty-five for up to thirty years to see whether eating fatty fish would reduce the risk of prostate cancer. The men were asked about diet, smoking habits, alcohol drinking, and physical activity. They were followed up between 1967 and 1997. Researchers calculated the number of cases of prostate cancer and deaths caused by the disease by consulting the Swedish National Cancer Register and National Death Register. During a thirty-year follow-up, four hundred sixty-six men were diagnosed with prostate cancer, and three hundred forty of these men died. The conclusion was that men who eat no fish have a two-fold to three-fold higher risk of prostate cancer than those who eat moderate or high amounts. Paul Terry says,:"Our study was done in Sweden, a country with traditionally high consumption of fatty fish from Northern (cold) waters, which contain high amounts of fatty acids." Since few dietary and other modifiable factors seem to be associated with lower risk of prostate cancer, our results may indicate an important means by which this disease might be prevented."

Essential fatty acids in fish inhibit the growth of prostate cancer cells in the lab and in experimental animals. But even earlier studies have found that the higher the concentration of fatty acids in man's bloodstream, the lower this risk of prostate cancer.

People in Sweden traditionally eat a lot of fatty fish from Northern (cold) waters, such a salmon, herring, and mackerel, which contain high amounts of fatty acids. The research was done at the Department of Medical Epidemiology, Karolinska Institute, Stockholm, Sweden.

Fish Oils

But there is more. Medical researchers in New Zealand provide convincing evidence that an increased consumption in fish oils helps reduce the risk of developing prostate cancer. Their study involved three hundred seventeen men who had been diagnosed with prostate cancer during 1996-1997 and four hundred eighty age-matched controls. Blood samples were obtained from all participants. Study participants who took fish oils were found to have a 40 percent lower incidence than those participants with levels in the lowest quartile.

(Norrish, A. E., Skeaff, C. M., Arribas, G. L., Sharpe, S. J., Jackson, R. T., British Journal of Cancer 1999 Dec, 81(7):1238-42).

GLA

Angiogenesis, the formation of new blood vessels, is an essential feature of malignant tumor development. *Gamma linolenic acid* (GLA) inhibits the growth and metastasis of a variety of tumor cells, including breast, prostate, and pancreatic cancer. GLA also has anti-metastatic effects.

Resveratol

Resveratrol works through more than a dozen different anticancer mechanisms and selectively targets cancer cells. This single supplement modulates hormones and has several mechanisms that stop cancer cells. Resveratrol is a substance found in grapes. It is also found in a plant called *polygonum cuspidatum*. It stops cancer cells from multiplying and even has the ability to destroy cancer cells. Research has found it has no side effects and can be administered orally. Additionally, it is inexpensive. So resveratrol is very toxic to cancer cells, but does not harm healthy cells.

Lignans

Flaxseed helps you fight prostate cancer. Mice that are fed plenty of flaxseed seemed to be protected against the worst forms of prostate cancer. Flaxseed is a rich source of fatty acids, fiber, and compounds known as *lignans,* all of which may play a role in protecting against cancer and perhaps also heart disease. A team at Duke University Medical Center fed large amounts of flaxseed to mice that were generically engineered to develop prostate cancer. They compared them to genetically engineered mice that were not fed any flaxseed. About 3 percent of the mice did not develop prostate cancer at all, and the rest had smaller tumors that were less likely to spread.

"Tumors in the untreated control group were twice the size of tumors in the flaxseed group." Dr. Xu Lin, who led the study, said in a statement.: "The tumors were also less aggressive in the flaxseed group, and two of the mice in the flaxseed group did not develop prostate cancer at all."

Other research has suggested that men who eat flaxseed have lower levels of prostate specific antigen, a protein produced by prostate cells that is now used as a test for prostate cancer. The higher levels, the more likely it is for a man to develop prostate cancer. "We are cautiously optimistic about these findings," urologist Wendy Demark-Wahnfried, who helped lead the study, said in a statement. "The amount of flaxseed given to each mouse was 5 percent of its food intake, which would be a very difficult amount for humans to eat, but it does signal that we are on the right track and need to continue research in this area." The team is now doing a study in men with prostate cancer.

Beta Glucan

Starting in the 1940's, researchers investigated the nutritional benefits of *beta glucan*. Derived from broken cell walls of yeasts, mushrooms, barley, and oats, beta glucans are capable of reducing unhealthy amounts of serum cholesterol and boosting the immune system. Beta glucan is a powerful immune stimulator, activating the *macrophages* in the immune system. Macrophages are white, large, and versatile immune cells. Studies have found this product not only has a positive action on the macrophages, but also on natural killer cells, too. In addition to these important functions, beta glucan is an effective antioxidant and free radical scavenger. Beta glucan is a safe, non-toxic, and orally effective supplement for those who wish to enhance their immune system and lower cholesterol levels.

IP6: Inositol Hexaphosphate

IP6 is a compound commonly found in fiber-rich plant foods. IP6 has been shown to shrink cancer tumors in laboratory. The National Cancer Institute is currently funding human trials.

Ellagic Acid

Ellagic acid is a compound found in berries. Research in animal and laboratory models has found that ellagic acid inhibits the growth of tumors caused by certain carcinogens. A number of double-blind studies in humans are under way to determine the effect of long-term daily consumption of concentrated raspberry extract on cancer cell activity in the human colon, prostate, and breast. A new publication called the "American Cancer Society's Guide to Complementary and Alternative Cancer Methods" has documented that ellagic acid is a very promising natural supplement, because it causes death of cancer cells in the lab without affecting normal healthy cells. Healthy cells have a normal life span of approximately one hundred twenty days before they undergo cell death. This process is called *apoptosis* (natural cell death). The body replaces these dying cells with new healthy cells. Conversely, cancer cells do not die. They multiply by division, making two cancer cells, then four, eight, sixteen, thirty-two, and so on. In lab tests, ellagic acid caused the cancer cells to go through the normal apoptosis process without damaging healthy cells. Chemotherapy, radiation, and most conventional treatments cause the death of cancer cells and healthy cells indiscriminately, while destroying the immune system. Ellagic acid is clearly the sensible choice.

AHCC: Actice Hexose Correlated Compound

AHCC is made from mushrooms. Various clinical trials conducted since 1987 in Japan have demonstrated that AHCC has the ability to support normal immune function and may improve the number and function of immune system cells. AHCC has been the subject of numerous clinical studies conducted at prestigious institutions, such as Hokkaido University, Kyorin University, and Teikyo University in Japan, and, in the United States, at Yale University and the Morehouse School of Medicine.

Maitake D -Fraction

Maitake D-fraction is a standardized extract from Maitake mushrooms, with special ingredients and compounds. This unique active compound makes it very potent in enhancing the immune system by oral administration. Because it is liquid, Maitake D-fraction can attain a much faster and much more effective absorption by one's body.

For the sake of scientific honesty, we should state that we left out a lot of information about those products, compounds, and ingredients because we would have to explain words, which would take whole books to explain in depth. But the main purpose of this booklet is application. If you are interested in finding out more, you can check our list of references at the end of this book to find more scientific information.

You now know that you can do a lot in relation to prostate cancer. There are many natural means to avoid it in the first place and to fight it when it is there.

Now you have the information.

Now you can act.

Today we are not helpless anymore when it comes to cancer. With every passing day, we learn more and get wiser about how to defeat this prominent enemy of mankind.

Action

Information: In the Far East (China, Japan) prostate cancer hardly exists. The reason is diet. What is wrong with the Western diet? Preserved meats, preserved vegetables, a lack of vegetables and fruits, chemically treated foods, excess sugar in all forms, and an excess of "bad" carbohydrates all make up our daily food intake.

Action: Correct these points begin with a really healthy diet.

Information: The following diet helps in relation to cancer: garlic, scallions, onions, plenty of fruit, and lots of vegetables— and everything should be organic.

Action: Change your diet accordingly.

Information: We need protein, good carbohydrates (complex carbohydrates), and good fats.

Action: Change your diet. Get your protein from soy, eat a lot of organic vegetables, and use cold -pressed organic olive oil and organic cold-pressed flax oil, for example.

Information: Prostate cancer fighters are found in Bok choy, broccoli, brussels sprouts, cabbage, cauliflower, collard greens, mustard seed, rutabaga, and turnips.

Action: Eat these vegetables on a regular basis.

Information: Too many "bad" starches, sugar, and fat cause high insulin levels. Low insulin is achieved by eating fruits, fiber, and vegetables.

Action: Cut your sugars, bad carbohydrates, and refined flours. Eat beans, vegetables, and fruits (remember they should be organic). Eat whole grain foods.

Information: Fiber helps prevent heart disease, diabetes, obesity, and cancer, including prostate cancer.

Action: Eat vegetables that are high in fiber, such as brussels sprouts, most beans, soybeans, apples, brown rice, and whole grains.

Information: Vitamins help against prostate cancer. Vitamin D is especially important. The best is a D vitamin called 1, 25 D.

Action: Take vitamin D 300 IU per day.

Information: Ultraviolet light helps create vitamin D.

Action: Get ten minutes of sun daily. The best time is up until 10 AM or after 4 PM.

Information: Exercise helps to fight cancer.

Action: Find the form of exercise that works for you. The best exercises are walking, running, swimming, and bicycling. Start slow and increase systematically.

Information: Avoiding stress (marital stress, employment stress, and environmental stress) helps prevent cancer.

Action: Prevent stress by solving problems with your spouse and children, and by creating a relaxed atmosphere in your home. At work, do not take more that what you can handle; say no when needed.

Information: Natural supplements can help with prostate cancer.

Balanced hormone levels (you need normal levels of free testosterone, low levels of estrogen (estradiol), and low levels of DHT. You need high levels of progesterone, DHEA, and pregnenolone.

Action: Balance your hormone levels with the following natural supplements:

testosterone cream, androstenedione, progesterone, DHEA, pregnenolone, Beta sitosterol, isoflavones, zinc, lignans, nettle root, saw palmetto, pygeum africanum, pumpkin seed oil, chrysin, DIM, eurycoma longifolia jack, tribulus terrestris, maca lepidium meyenii G, and muira puama.

Information: Antioxidants help with prostate cancer.

Action: Take selenium, vitamin E, lycopene, EFA, GLA, flax oil, Resveratrol, and drink green tea.

Information: Immune system boosters help.

Action: Take beta glucan, IP6, Ellagic acid, AHCC, and Maitake D-fraction.

Information: Angiogenesis inhibitors can help with prostate cancer.

Action:

Use angiogenesis inhibitors

Convolvulus arvensis and shark cartilage are two natural sources with anti- angiogenesis effect.

References

Adhami,V. M., Siddiqui, I.A.,Ahmad, N., Gupta, S., Mukhtar, H. Department of Dermatology, University of Wisconsin, Madison,Wisconsin Oral consumption of green tea polyphenols inhibits insulin-like growth factor-I-induced signaling in an autochthonous mouse model of prostate cancer. *Cancer Res.* 2004 Dec 1. 64(23): 8715–22.

Adriazola, Semino, M. Lozano, Otega J. L., Garcia, C., et al. Symptomatic treatment of benign hypertropy of the prostate. Comparative study of prazosin and serenoa repens. *Arch Esp Urol 1992.* 45: 211–3.

Agarwal, C., Dhanalakshmi, S., Singh, R. P., Agarwal, R. Department of Pharmaceutical Sciences, School of Pharmacy, University of Colorado Cancer Center, University of Colorado Health Sciences Center, Denver, CO. Inositol hexaphosphate inhibits growth and induces G1 arrest and apoptotic death of androgen-dependent human prostate carcinoma LNCaP cells. *Neoplasia.* 2004 Sep-Oct. 6(5): 646–59.

Agarwal, C., Dhanalakshmi, S., Singh, R.P., Agarwal, R. Department of Pharmaceutical Sciences, School of Pharmacy, University of Colorado Health Sciences Center, Denver, Colorado. Inositol hexaphosphate inhibits constitutive activation of NF- kappa B in androgen-inde-pendent human prostate carcinoma DU145 cells. *Anticancer Res.* 2003 Sep-Oct. 23(5A): 3855–61.

Aggarwal, B. B.,Takada,Y., Oommen, O.V.The University of Texas M.D. Anderson Cancer Center, Cytokine Research Section, Department of Experimental Therapeutics, P.O. Box 143, 1515 Holcombe Boulevard,
Houston,Texas. From chemoprevention to chemotherapy: common targets and common goals. *Expert Opin Investig Drugs.* 2004 Oct 13. (10): 1327–38.

American Cancer Society's Guide to Complementary and Alternative Cancer Methods. Published by the American Cancer Society 2000.

Andro, M. -C., Riffaud, J. -P. Pygeum africanum extract for the treatment of patients with benign prostatic hyperplasia:A review of 25 years of published experience. *Curr TherRes.* 1995. 56: 796 [review].

Ansari, M. S., Gupta, N. P. Department of Urology,All India Institute of Medical Sciences, New Delhi 110029,India. Lycopene: a novel drug therapy in hormone refractory metastatic prostate cancer. *Urol Oncol.* 2004 Sep–Oct. 22(5): 415-20.

Antunes, E., Gordo,W. M., de Oliveira,J. F.,Teixeira, C. E., Hyslop, S., De Nucci, G. Department of Pharmacology, Faculty of Medical Sciences, UNICAMP.The relaxation of isolated rabbit corpus cavernosum by the herbal medicine Catuama and its constituents. *Phytother Res.* 2001 Aug. 15. (5): 416-21.

Arnot, Bob.The Prostate Cancer Protection Plan. New York: Little, Brown, and Co., 2000.

Augustsson, K., Michaud, D. S., Rimm, E. B., Leitzmann, M. F., Stampfer, M. J.,Willett,W. C., Giovannucci, E. Department of Nutrition, Harvard School of Public Health, Harvard Medical School, Boston.A prospective study of intake of fish and marine fatty acids and prostate cancer. *Cancer Epidemiol Biomarkers Prev.* 2003 Jan. 12. (1): 64-7.

Authie, D., Cauquil J. Evaluation of the efficacy ofpermixon in daily practice. *Comptes Rendus de Therap.* 1987. 56: 1-9.

Aziz, M. H., Kumar, R.,Ahmad, N. Cancer chemoprevention by resveratrol: in vitro and in vivo studies and the underlying mechanisms (review). *IntJOncol.* 2003 July 23. (I): 17--28.

Bach, D., Ebeling, L. Long-term drug treatment of benign prostatic hyperplasia --—results of a protective 3-year multicenter study using Sabal extract IDS 89. *Phytomed.* 1996.3: 105-11, (originally published in *Urologe* [B]) 1995. 35: 178--83.

Bachrach, U., Shayovitz,A., Marom,Y., Ramu,A., Ramu, N. Omithine decarboxylase—a predictor for tumor chemosensitivity. *Cell MolBiol (Noisy-le-grand).* 1994 Nov.; 40(7): 957--64.

Bemis, D. L., Capodice,J. L., Desai, M., Buttyan, R., Katz,A. E.A concentrated aglycone isoflavone preparation (GCP) that demonstrates potent anti prostate cancer activity in vitro and in vivo. *Clin Cancer Res.* 2004 Aug 1. 10(15): 5282-92.

Bennett, B. C., Hicklin, J. R. Uses of saw palmetto in Florida. *Economic Botany.* 1998.

Blumenthal, M.T., Busse,W. R., Goldberg,A., et al.The Complete German Commission E Monographs. *Therapeutic Guide to Herbal Medicines.* American Botanical Council.Austin,TX. 1998.

Boccafoschi, C.,Annoscia, S. Confromto fra estratto di Serenoa repens e placebo mediate prova clinica controllata in pazienti con adenomatosi prostatica. *Urologia.* 1983.

Bohm, V., Bitsch, R. Intestinal absorption of lycopene from different matrices and interactions to other carotenoids, the lipid status, and the antioxidant capacity of human plasma. *Eur J Nutr.* 1999 June. 38(3): 118–25.

Bombardelli, E., Marrazzoni, M. Unpublished information conducted at the University of Pavia. Provided by Indena Corp. Milan, Italy. 1997.

Bosetti, C., Talamini, R., Montella, M., Negri, E., Conti, E., Franceschi, S., La Vecchia, C. Istituto di Ricerche Farmacologiche "Mario Negri." Milan, Italy. Retinol, carotenoids and the risk of prostate cancer: A case-control study from Italy. Int J Cancer. 2004 Nov. 20. 112(4): 689.

Botanical Ad Hoc Advisory Panel Comments. February 1999.

Braeckman, J., Denis, L., de Laval, J., et al. A double-blind, placebo-controlled study of the plant extract serenoa repens in the treatment of benign hyperplasia of the prostate. *Eur J Clin Res.* 1997. 9: 247–59.

Braeckman, J. The extract of serenoa repens in the treatment of benign prostatic hyperplasia: a multicenter open study. *Curr Ther Res.* 1994. 55: 776–85.

Breau, W., Stadler, F., Hagenlocher, M., et al. Der Sabalfrucht-extrakt SG 291. Ein phytotherapeutikumzur behandlung der benignen prostatahyperplasie. *Zeitschrift fur Phytotherapie 1992*, 13: 107-15.

Briley, M., Carilla, E., Roger, A. Inhibitory effect of Permixon on Testosterone 5D-reductase activity of the rat ventral prostate. Br J Pharmacol. 1984. 83: 40 IP.

Browner, W. S., Kahn, A. J., Ziv, E., Reiner, A. P., Oshima, J., Cawthon, R. M., Hsueh, W. C., Cummings, S. R. The genetics of human longevity. California Pacific Medical Center Research Institute, San Francisco, CA. US Am J Med. 2004 Dec 1. 117(11): 882–3.

Brownson, R. C., J. C. Chang, J. R. Davis, et al. Physical activity on the job and cancer in Missouri. American Journal of Public Health. 1991. 81: 639.

Brusselmans, K., De Schrijver, E., Heyns, W., Verhoeven, G., Swinnen, J. V. Laboratory for Experimental Medicine and Endocrinology, Department of Developmental Biology, Gasthuisberg, Catholic University of Leuven, Belgium. Epigallocatechin-3-gallate is a potent natural inhibitor of fatty acid synthase in intact cells and selectively induces apoptosis in prostate cancer cells. *Int J Cancer* 2003 Oct 10. 106(6): 856–62.

Brusselmans, K., Vrolix, R., Verhoeven, G., Swinnen, J. V. Induction of cancer cell apoptosis by flavonoids is associated with their ability to inhibit fatty acid synthase activity. *J Biol Chem.* 2005 Feb. 18. 280(7): 5636–45.

Campos, M. M., Fernandes, E. S., Ferreira, J., Bortolanza, L. B., Santos, A. R., Calixto, J. B., Department of Pharmacology, Centre of Biological Sciences, Universidade Federal de Santa Catarina, Rua Ferreira Lima, 82, 88015-420, Florianopolis, SC, Brazil. Pharmacological and neurochemical evidence for antidepressant-like effects of the herbal product Catuama. *Pharmacol Biochem Behav.* 2004 Aug. 78(4): 757–64.

Carilla, E., Briley, M., Fauran, F., et al. Binding of permixon, a new treatment for prostatic benign hyperplasia, to the cytosolic androgen receptor in the rat prostate. *J Steroid Biochem.* 1984. 20(1): 21--3.

Carraro, J. C., Raynaud, J. P., Koch, G., et al. Comparison of phytotherapy (Permixon®) with finasteride in the treatment of benign prostate hyperplasia: a randomized international study of 1,098 patients. *Prostate.* 1996. 29: 231–40.

Carreras, J. O. Experience with the hexane extract of serenoa repens in the treatment of benign prostate hyperplasia. *Arch Esp de Urol.* 1987. 40(5): 310–3.

Carruthers, Malcom. The Testosterone Revolution. (Thorsons)

Casarosa, C., di Coscio, M. C., Fratte, M. Lack of effects of a lyposterolic extract of *serenoa repens* on plasma levels of testosterone, follicle-stimulating hormone, and luteinizing hormone. *Clin Ther.* 1988. 10(5): 585–8.

Chacon, Gloria de Popovici. Maca The Peruvian Food Plant, with Highly Nutritional and Medicinal Properties. Lima, Peru. 2002.

Champault, G., Patel, J. C., Bonnard, A. M. A double-blind trial of an extract of the plant serenoa repens in benign prostatic hyperplasia. *Br J Clin Pharmacol.* 1984. 18: 461–2.

Chan, J. M., Stampfer, M. J., Ma, J., Gann, P. H., Gaziano, J. M., Giovannucci, E. L. Dairy products, calcium, and prostate cancer risk in the Physicians' Health Study. *Am J Clin Nutr.* 2001 Oct. 74(4): 549–54.

Chang, Y. C., Riby, J., Chang, G. H., Peng, B. C., Firestone, G., Bjeldanes, L. F. Cytostatic and antiestrogenic effects of 2-(indol-3-ylmethyl)-3,3'-diindolylmethane, a major i vivo product of dietary indole-3-carbinol. *Biochem Pharmacol.* 1999.

Chatelain, C., Autet, W., Brackman, F. Comparison of once and twice daily dosage forms of Pygeum africanum extract in patients with benign prostatic hyperplasia: a randomized, double-blind study, with long-

term open label extension. *Urology.* 1999. 54: 473-8.
Chemoprevention Working Group to the American Association for Cancer Research. Prevention of cancer in the next millennium: report of the Chemoprevention Working Group to the American Association for Cancer Research. *Cancer Res.* 1999 October 1. 59(19): 4743-58.

Chevalier, G., Benard, P., Cousse, H., et al. Distribution study of radioactivity in rats after oral administration of the lipido/sterolic extract ot *serenoa repens* (Permixon®) *Eur J Drug Metab Pharmacokinet.* 1997. 22(1): 73-83.

Chinni, S. R., Li, Y., Upadhyay, S., Koppolu, P. K., Sarkar, F. H. Indole-3-carbinol (I3C) induced cell growth inhibition, Gl cell cycle arrest and apoptosis in prostate cancer cells. *Oncogene.* 2001 May 24. 20(23): 2927-36.

Chisaka, T., et al. *Chemical and Pharmaceutical Bulletin,* Tokyo, 1988.

Cohen, J. H., Kristal, A. R., Stanford, J. L. Fruit and vegetable intakes and prostate cancer risk. *JNati Cancer Inst.* 2000 Jan. 5. 92(1): 61-8.

Confronto dellaefficacia delPestratto di Serenoa repens (Permixon®) versus l'estratto di Pigeum africanum e placebo. *Urologia.* 1983. 50: 752-8.

Cristoni, A., Morazzoni, P., Bombardelli, E. Chemical and pharmacological study on hypercritical C02 extracts of serenoa repens fruits. Fitoterapia. 1997. 68(4): 355-8.

Cukier, J., Ducassou, J., Le Guillou, M., et al. Pennixon® versus placebo. Resultats d'une etude multicentrque. *CR Ther Pharmacol Clin.* 1985. 4(25): 15-21.

Dagnelie, P. C., Schuurman, A. G., Goldbohm, R. A., Van den Brandt, P. A. Department of Epidemiology, Maastricht University, Maastricht, The Netherlands. Diet, anthropometric measures and prostate cancer risk: a review of prospective cohort and intervention studies. *BJU Int.* 2004 May. 93(8): 1139-50.

Damianaki, A., Bakogeorgou, E., Kampa, M., et al. Potent inhibitory action of red wine polyphenols on human breast cancer cells. *J Cell Biochem.* 2000 June 6. 78(3): 429-41.

Da Silva, A. L., Piato, A. L., Bardini, S., Netto, C. A., Nunes, D. S., Elisabetsky, E. Laboratorio de Etnofarmacologia, ICBS, Universidade Federal do Rio Grande do Sul, Av. Sarmento Leite 500/202, 90046-900 Porto Alegre, RS, Brazil. Memory retrieval improvement by ptychopetalum olacoides in young and aging mice. *J Ethnopharmacol.* 2004 Dec. 95(2-3): 199-203.

Dathe, G., Schmid H. Phytotherapy of benign prostatic hyperplasia (BPH) with extractum serenoa repens. *Urolog B.* 1991. 31: 220-3.

David, R. D., Grunberger, I., Shore, N., Swierzewski, S. J. 3rd. Multicenter initial U.S. experience with CoreTherm-monitored feedback transurethral microwave thermotherapy for individualized treatment of patients with symptomatic benign prostatic hyperplasia. *J Endourol.* 2004 Sep. 18. (7): 682-5.

De Bemardi, Di Valserra, M., Tripodi, A. S., Contos, S., et al. Serenoa repens capsules: a bioequivalence study. *Acta Toxicol Ther.* 1994. 15(1): 21-39.

De La Rosette, J. J., Floratos, D. L., Severens, J. L., Kiemeney, L.A., Debruyne, F. M., Pilar Laguna, M. Transurethral resection vs microwave thermotherapy of the prostate: a cost-consequences analysis. *BJU Int.* 2003 Nov. 92(7): 713-8.

Delos, S., Carsol, J. L., Ghazarossian, E., et al. Testosterone metabolism in primary cultures of human prostate epithelial cells and fibroblasts. *J Steroid Biochem.* 1995.

Demark-Wahnefried, W., Robertson, C. N., Walther, P. J., Polascik, T. J., Paulson, D. F., Vollmer, R. T. Division of Urologic Surgery, Duke University Medical Center, Durham, NC. *Urology.* 2004 May. 63(5): 900-4.

Denis, L. G. Comparison of phytotherapy (Pennixon®) with finasteride in the treatment of benign prostate hyperplasia: a randomized international study of 1098 patients [editorial review]. *Prostate.* 1996. 29(3): 241-2.

Descotes, J. L., Rambeaud, J. J., Deschaseaux, P., et al. Placebo-controlled evaluation of the efficacy and tolerability of Permixon® in benign prostatic hyperplasia after exclusion of placebo responders. *Clin Drug Invest.* 1995. 9: 291-7.

De Swaef, S. I., Vlietinck, A. J. Simultaneous quantitation of lauric acid and ethyl laurate in Sabal serrulata by capillary gas chromatography and derivatisation with trimethyl sulphoniumhydroxide. *J. Chromatogr A.* 1996. 719: 479-82.

DeVere White, R. W., Hackman, R. M., Soares, S. E., Beckett, L. A., Li, Y., Sun, B. Effects of a genistein-rich extract on PSA levels in men with a history of prostate cancer.
Urology. 2004 Feb. 63(2): 259-63.

Dhanalakshmi, S., Agarwal, R., Agarwal, C. Inhibition of NF-kappaB pathway in grape-seed extract-induced apoptotic death of human prostate carcinoma DU145 cells. Int Joncol. 2003 Sep. 23(3): 721-7.

Diiker, E. M., Kopanski, L., Schweikert, H. U. Inhibition of 5D-Reductase Activity by Extracts from Sabal Serrulata. Braunschweig, 37th Annual Congress on Medicinal Plant Research. September 1989.

Di Silverio, F., Monti, S., Sciarra, A., et al. Effects of long-term treatment with Serenoa repens (Pennixon®) on the concentrations and regional distribution of Androgens and epidermal growth factor in benign prostatic hyperplasia. *Prostate.* 1998. 37: 77--83.

DiSilverio, F., D'Eramo, G., Lubrano, C., et al. Evidence that serenoa repens extract displays an anti-estrogenic activity in prostatic tissue of benign prostatic hypertrophy patients. *Eur Urol.* 1992. 21: 309–14.

Djuric, Z., Powell, L. C. Antioxidant capacity of lycopene-containing foods. *Int J Food Sci Nutr.* 2001 Mar. 52(2): 143–9.

Donaldson, M. S. Nutrition and cancer: A review of the evidence for an anti-cancer diet. *Nutr J.* 2004 Oct. 20. 3(1): 19 [Epub ahead of print]

Dorai, T., Aggarwal, B. B. Comprehensive Cancer Center, Our Lady of Mercy Medical Center, New York Medical College, Bronx, NY. Role of chemopreventive agents in cancer therapy. Cancer Lett. 2004 Nov. 25. 215(2): 129–40.

Dubuisson, J. G., Dyess, D. L., Gaubatz, J. W. Resveratrol modulates human mammary epithelial cell 0-acetyltransferase, sulfo transferase, and kinase activation of the het-erocyclic amine carcinogen N-hydroxy-PhIP. *Cancer Lett.* 2002 Aug. 8. 182(1): 27–32.

Elattar, T. M., Virji, A. S. Modulating effect of resveratrol and quercetin on oral cancer cell growth and proliferation. *Anticancer Drugs.* 1999 Feb. 10(2): 187–93.

Ellingwood, F., Lloyd, J. U. American materia medica, therapeutics, and pharmacognosy Volume II. 1919 Portland: Eclectic Medical Publications. 457-9. Reprinted 1998.

El-Sheikh, M. M., Dakkad, M. R., Saddique, A. The effect of permixon on androgen receptors. *Acta Obstet Gynecol Scand.* 1988. 67: 397-9.

Emili, E., Lo Cigno, M., Petrone, U. Risultati clinici su un nuovo farmaco nella terapia dell'ipertrofiadellaprostata (Permixon®). *Urologia.* 1983. 50: 1042-8.

Epel, E. S., Blackburn, E. H., Lin, J., Dhabhar, F. S., Adler, N. E., Morrow, J. D., Cawthon, R. M. Accelerated telomere shortening in response to life stress. *Proc Natl Acad Sci USA.* 2004 Dec. 7. 101(49): 17312-5. The expression of autocrine growth modulators in human breast cancer cells. *Antioxid Redox Signal.* 2001 Dec. 3(6): 969-79.

Fang, M. Z., Wang, Y., Ai, N., Hou, Z., Sun, Y., Lu, H., Welsh, W., Yang, C. S., Department of Chemical Biology, Ernest Mario School of Pharmacy,

Rutgers, The State University of New Jersey, 164 Frelinghuysen Road, Piscataway, NJ. Tea polyphenol (-)-epigallocatechin-3-gallate inhibits DNA methyltransferase and reactivates methylation-silenced genes in cancer cell lines. *Cancer Res.* 2003 Nov. 15. 63(22): 7563-70

Fang, N., Casida, J. E. Anticancer action of cube insecticide: correlation for rotenoid constituents between inhibition of NADH: ubiquinone oxidoreductase and induced omithine decarboxylase activities. *Proc Natl Acad Sci USA.* 1998 Mar. 31. 95(7): 3380-4.

Felter, H. W., Lloyd, J. U. Kings's American Dispensatory Volume II, eighteenth edition .1898. 1750-2. Reprinted 1994.

Felter, H. W. The eclectic materia medica, pharmacology, and therapeutics. Volume I.

Festa, F., et al. Strong antioxidant activity of ellagic acid in mammalian cells in vitro revealed by the comet assay. *Anticancer Res.* 2001. 21: 3903-8.

Gallagher, R. P., Kutynec, C. L. Diet, micronutrients, and prostate cancer: a review of the evidence. *Can J Urol.* 1997 Jun. 4(2 Supp 1): 22-27.

Gambelunghe C, Rossi R, Sommavilla M, Ferranti C, Rossi R, Ciculi C, Gizzi S, Micheletti A, Rufini S. Department of Clinical and Experimental Medicine, Division of Sports Medicine-Laboratorio delle Attivita Motorie e Sportive, University of Perugia, Perugia, Italy J Med Food. 2003 Winter;6(4):387-90

Gann, P. H., C. H. Hennekens, J. Ma, et al. A prospective study of sex hormone levels and risk of prostate cancer. *Journal of the National Cancer Institute.* 1996. 88.

Gann, P.H., M. L. Daviglus, A. R. Dyer, et al. Heart rate and prostate cancer mortality: Results of a prospective analysis. *Cancer Epidemiology, Biomarkers, and Prevention.* 1995. 4: 611-16.

Garfinkel, L. Variations in mortality by weight men and women. *Journal of Chronic Diseases.* 32.

Gerber, G. S., Zagaja, G. P., Bales, G. T., et al. Saw palmetto (serenoa repens) in men with lower urinary tract symptoms: Effects on urodynamic parameters and voiding symptoms. *Urology.* 1998. 51: 1003-7.

Gerhauser, C., Lee. S. K., Kosmeder, J. W., et al. Regulation ofomithine decarboxylase induction by deguelin, a natural product cancer chemopreventive agent. *Cancer Res.* 1997 Aug. 15. 57(16): 3429-35.

Ghosh, J., C. E. Myers. Inhibition of arachidonate 5-lipoxygenase triggers massive apoptosis in human prostate cancer cells. *Proceedings of the National Academy of Sciences of the USA.* 1998 Oct. 27. 95(22): 13182-7.

Giovannucci, E., E. B. Rimm, G.A. Colditz, et al.,A Prospective Study of Dietary Fat and Risk of Prostate Cancer. *Journal of the National Cancer Institute.* 1993 Oct. 6. 85(19): 571-9.

Giovannucci, E.,Ascherio,A., Rimm, E. B., Stampfer, M. J., Colditz, G.A., Willett,W. C. Intake of carotenoids and retinol in relation to risk of prostate cancer.*J Natl Cancer Inst.* 1995. 87: 1767-76.

Glaser, R., J. K. Kiecolt-Glaser, P.T. Marucha, et al. Stress-related changes in proinflammatory cytokine production wounds. *Archives of General Psychiatry.* 1999 May. 56: 450.

Glaser, R., J. K. Kiecolt-Glaser, R. H. Bonneau, et al. Stress-induced modulation of the immune response to recombina Hepatitis B-vaccine. *Psychosomatic Medicine.* 1992. 54: 22.

Globocan 2000: cancer incidence, mortality and prevalence worldwide [CD-ROM]. International Agency for Research on Cancer,World Health Organization: 2001.

Godley, P.A., M. K. Campbell, P. Gallagher, et al. Biomarkers of essential fatty acid consumption and risk of prostatic carcinoma. *Cancer Epidemiology, Biomarkers, and Prevention.* 1996 Nov. 5(11): 889-95.

Goepel, M., Hecker, U., Krege, S., et al. Saw palmetto extracts potently and noncompetitively inhibit human alpha 1-adrenoceptors in vitro. *Prostate.* 1999. 38(3): 208-15.

Gonzalez-Suarez, E., Geserick, C., Flores, J. M., Blasco, M.A. Antagonistic effects of telomerase on cancer and aging in K5-mTert transgenic mice. *Oncogene.* 2005 Jan. 31.

Grasso, M., Montesano,A., Buonaguidi,A., et al. Comparative effects of alfuzosin versus serenoa repens in the treatment of symptomatic benign prostatic hyperplasia. *Arch Esp Urol.* 1995. 48: 97-103.

Gravas, S., Laguna, M. P., De La Rosette, J. J. Application of external microwave thermotherapy in urology: past, present, and future.*J Endourol.* 2003 Oct. 17(8): 659-66.

Greenwald P. Clinical trials in cancer prevention: current results and perspectives for the future. *J Nutr.* 2004 Dec. 134(12 Suppl): 3507S-3512S.

Gruenwald, J. History of saw palmetto and its use. Presentation at the International Saw Palmetto Symposium. August 1998. American Herbal Products Association. Naples, Florida. 1998.

Gutierrez, M., Garcia de Boto, M. J., Cantabrana, B., et al. Mechanisms involved in the spasmolytic effect of extracts from Sabal serrulata fruit on smooth muscle. *Gen Pharmacol.* 1996. 27(1): 171-6.

Gutierrez, M., Hidalgo, A., Cantabrana, B. Spasmolytic activity of a lipidic extract from Sabal serrulata fruits: further study of the mechanisms underlying this activity. *Planta Medica*. 1996. 62: 507-11.

Halls, L. K. *Saw palmetto/serenoa repens* (Bartr.) Small [Woody plants as wildlife food, species]. USDA. U.S. Southern Forest Experiment Station. 1977. FO. 15: 93-4. Map.

Hagenlocher, M., Romaic, G., Schweikert, H. U. Specific inhibition of 5D-reductase by a new extract of sabal serrulata. *Akt Urol*. 1993. 24: 146-9.

Harrison's Principles of Internal Medicine. 15th edition. New York. Mc Graw-Hill. 2001.

Harte, Jane L., Georg H. Eifert. The effect of running, environment, and attentional focus on athletes' catecholamin and cortisol levels and mood. *Psychophysiology*, 32, (1995): 49-54.

Harvei, S., K. S. Bjerve, S. Tretii, et al. Prediagnostic level of fatty acids in serum phosphohpids: Omega-3 and Omega-6 fatty acids and the risk of prostate cancer. *International Journal of Cancer*. 1997 May 16. 71(4): 545-51.

Haussmann, M. F., Winkler, D. W., Huntington, C. E., Nisbet, I. C., Vleck, C. M. Telomerase expression is differentially regulated in birds of differing life span. *Ann N Y Acad Sci*. 2004 Jun. 1019: 186-90.

Hayes. R. Dietary factors and risk for prostate cancer among blacks and whites. *Cancer Epidemiology, Biomarkers, and Prevention*. 1999 Jan.

Heber, D., Lu, Q. Y., Go, V. L. Role of tomatoes, tomato products, and lycopene in cancer prevention. *Adv Exp Med Biol*. 2001. 492: 29-37.

Hoffman, R. M., MacDonald, R., Wilt, T. J. Laser prostatectomy for benign prostatic obstruction. *Cochrane Database Syst Rev*. 2004. (1): CD001987.

Hovenanian, M. S., C. D. Deming. The heterologous growth of cancer of the human prostate. *Surgery Gynecology and Obstetrics*. 1948. 86: 29-35.

Hryb, D. J., Khan, M. S., Romas, N. A., Rosner, W. The effect of extracts of the roots of the stinging nettle (Urtica dioica) on the interaction of SHBG with its receptor on human prostatic membranes. *Planta Med*. 1995 Feb. 61(1): 31-2.

Hsieh, T. C., Wu, J. M. Grape-derived chemo preventive agent resveratrol decreases prostate-specific antigen (PSA) expression in LNCaP cells by an Androgen receptor (AR)-independent mechanism. *Anticancer Res*. 2000 Jan-Feb. 20(1A): 225-8.

Hudson, E.A., Howells, L. M., Gallacher-Horiey, B., Fox, L. H., Gescher, A., Manson, M. M. Growth-inhibitory effects of the chemopreventive agent indole-3-carbinol are increased in combination with the polyamine putrescine in the SW480 colon tumour cell line. *BMC Cancer.* 2003 Jan. 14. 3(1): 2.

Huidobro, C., Bolmsjo, M., Larson, T., de la Rosette, J., Wagrell, L., Schelin, S., Gorecki, T., Mattiasson, A. Evaluation of microwave thermotherapy with histopathology, magnetic resonance imaging, and temperature mapping. *J Urol.* 2004 Feb. 171(2 Pt 1): 672-8.

Hurley, T. G., B. C. Olendzki, et al. Nutri-economic factors in relation to prostate cancer. *European Urology.* 1992. 21: 309-14.

Hussain, M., Banerjee, M., Sarkar, F. H., Djuric, Z., Pollak, M. N., Doerge, D., Fontana, J., Chinni, S., Davis, J., Forman, J., Wood, D. P., Kucuk, O. Soy isoflavones in the treatment of prostate cancer. *Nutr Cancer* 2003. 47(2): 111-7.

Hussain, T., Gupta, S., Adhami, V. M., Mukhtar, H.,
University of Wisconsin, Department of Dermatology, 1300 University Ave., Madison, WI. Green tea constituent epigallocatechin-3-gallate selectively inhibits COX-2 without affecting COX-1 expression in human prostate carcinoma cells. *Int J Cancer.* 2005 Feb. 10. 113(4): 660-9.

Hwang, E. S., Bowen, P. E., Department of Human Nutrition, University of Illinois, Chicago.
Cell cycle arrest and induction of apoptosis by lycopene in LNCaP human prostate cancer cells. J Med Food. 2004 Fall. 7(3): 284-9.

In men, progesterone inhibits the harmful effects of excess estrogen. *Der Spiegel.* 2003 April 4. (Based on the world-congress in Berlin about aging, August 2003.)

Jeong HJ, Shin YG, Kim IH, Pezzuto JM. Inhibition of aromatase activity by flavonoids. Department of Medicinal Chemistry and Pharmacognosy, College of Pharmacy, University of Illinois at Chicago. Arch Pharm Res. 1999 Jun;22(3):309-12.

Jian, L., Du, C. J., Lee, A. H., Binns, C. W. School of Public Health, Curtin University of Technology, Perth, Australia. Do dietary lycopene and other carotenoids protect against prostate cancer? Int J Cancer. 2004 Oct. 28.

Jian, L., Xie, L. P., Lee, A. H., Binns, C. W. School of Public Health, Curtin University of Technology, Perth, WA, Australia. Protective effect of green tea against prostate cancer: a case-control study in southeast China. *Int J Cancer.* 2004 Jan 1. 108(1): 130-5.

Jain, M. G., Hislop, G.T., Howe, G. R., Ghadirian, P. Plant foods, antioxidants, and prostate cancer risk: findings from case-control studies in Canada. *Nutr Cancer.* 1999. 34(2): 173–84.

Jang, M., Cai, L., Udeani, G. O., et al. Cancer chemopreventive activity of resveratrol, a natural product derived from grapes. *Science.* 1997 Jan. 10. 275(5297): 218–20.

Jankun, J., Selman, S. H., Swiercz, R., Skrzypczak-Jankun, E., Department of Urology, Medical College of Ohio, Toledo. Why drinking green tea could prevent cancer. *Nature.* 1997 Jun. 5. 387(6633): 561.

Jellinck, P. H., Newcombe, A. M., Forkert, P. G., Martucci, C. P. Distinct forms of hepatic androgen 6 beta-hydroxylase induced in t rat by indole-3-carbinol and pregnenolon carbonitrile. *JSteroid Biochem Mol Biol.* 1994 Nov. 51(3-4): 219–25.

Kampa, M., Hatzoglou, A., Notas, G., et al. Wine antioxidant polyphenols inhibit the proliferation of human prostate cancer cell lines. *Nutr Cancer.* 2000. 37(2): 223–33.

Kaplan, S. A. Reduction of rat prostate weight by combined quercetin-finasteride treatment is associated with cell cycle deregulation. *J Urol.* 2005 Mar. 173(3): 914.

Kao YC, Zhou C, Sherman M, Laughton CA, Chen S. Molecular basis of the inhibition of human aromatase (estrogen synthetase) by flavone and isoflavone phytoestrogens: A site-directed mutagenesis study. Environ Health Perspect. 1998 Feb;106(2):85-92.

Kiecolt-Glaser, J. K., J. R. Dura, C. E. Speicher, et al. Spousal caregivers of dementia victims: longitudinal changes in immunity and health. *Psychosomatic Medicine.* 1991. 53: 345–62.

Kiecolt-Glaser, J. K., W. B. Malarkey, M. Chee, et al. Negative behavior during marital conflict is associated with immunological down-regulation. *Psychosomatic Medicine.* 1993. 55: 395–9.

Kiecolt-Glaser, J. K., W. Gamer, C. E. Speicher, et al. Psychosocial modifiers of immunocompetence in medical students. *Psychosomatic Medicine.* 1984. 46: 7-14

Kiecolt-Glaser, J. K., P.T. Marucha, W. B. Malarkey, et al. Slowing of wound healing by psychological stress. *Lancet,* 34, (November 4, 1995): 1194-6.

Kiecolt-Glaser, J. K., R. Glaser, J.T. Cacioppo, et al. Marital conflict in older adults: Endocrinological and immunological correlates. *Psychosomatic Medicine,* 59, (1997): 339-49.

Kiecolt-Glaser, J. K., R. Glaser, S. Gravenstein, et al. Chronic stress alters the immune response to influenza virus vaccine in older adults. *Proceedings of the National Academy Sciences of the USA,* 93, (April 1996): 3043-7.

Klatz, Ronald M.D., Dr. Robert Goldman. "The New Anti-Aging Revolution." North Bergen, NJ: Basics Health Pub. Inc., 2003.

Klatz, Ronald, M.D. "Ten Weeks to a Younger You." Chicago, IL: Sport Tech lLabs Inc., 1999.

Klatz, Ronald M.D., Dr. Robert Goldman. "Seven Anti-Aging Secrets." Chicago, IL: Elite Sport Medicine Pub, 1996.

Koenig, et al. Does religious attendance prolong six-year follow-up study of 3,968 older adults. *Gerontology.* 1999 July. 54A: 370-7

Kolonel, L. N., Hankin, J. H., Whittemore, A. S., et al. Vegetables, fruits, legumes, and prostate cancer: a multiethnic case-control study. *Cancer Epidemiol Biomarkers Prev.* 2000 Aug.; 9(8): 795--804.

Kondas, J., Philipp, V., Dioszeghy, G. Sabal serrulata extract (Strogen forte®) in the treatment of symptomatic benign prostatic hyperplasia. *Int Urol Nephrol. 1996.* 28: 767-72.

Kristal, A. R., Lampe, J. W. Brassica vegetables and prostate cancer risk: a review of the epidemiological evidence. *Nutr Cancer.* 2002. 42(1): 1-9.

Krzeski, T., Kazon, M., Borkowski, A., et al. Combined extracts of urtica dioica and pygeum africanum in the treatment of benign prostatic hyperplasia: Double-blind comparison of two doses, *din Ther.* 1993. 15: 1011-20.

Kumar, N. B., Cantor, A., Allen, K., Riccardi, D., Besterman-Dahan, K., Seigne, J., Helal, M., Salup, R., Pow-Sang, J. The specific role of isoflavones in reducing prostate cancer risk. *Prostate.* 2004 May 1. 59(2): 141-7.

Kurth, H. Saw palmetto extracts- standardization, characterization, & analytical comparison of finished products. Presentation at the 1998 International Saw Palmetto Symposium. American Herbal Products Assoc. Naples, Florida. 1998.

Lambert, J. D., Hong, J., Yang, G. Y., Liao, J., Yang, C. S. Inhibition of carcinogenesis by polyphenols: evidence from laboratory investigations. *Am J Clin Nutr.* 2005 Jan. 81(1 Suppl): 284S-291S.

Lansky, E. P., Harrison, G., Froom, P., Jiang, W. G. Pomegranate (punica granatum) pure chemicals show possible synergistic inhibition of human PC-3 prostate cancer cell invasion across Matrigeltrade mark. *Invest New Drugs.* 2005 Jan. 23(2): 121-2.

Larsen, Reed, P. M.D., Henry Kronennberg, M.D., Shlomo Melmed, M.D.,

Kenneth S. Polonsky, M.D. *Williams Textbook of Endocrinology.* Tenth ed. Philadelphia: Saunders, 2003.

Lazarou, J., BM Pomeranz, PN Corey. Incidence of Adverse Drug Reactions in hospitalized patients: A Meta-Analysis of prospective studies. JAMA 1998 279: 1200-5.

Le, H.T,, Schaldach, C. M., Firestone, G. L., Bjeldanes, L. F. Plant-derived 3,3'-Di-Indolyl Methaneis a strong Androgen antagonist in human prostate cancer cells *Biol Chem.* 2003 Jun 6. 278(23): 21136-45.

Lechel, A., Satyanarayana, A., Ju, Z., Plentz, R. R., Schaetzlein, S., Rudolph, C., Wilkens, L., Wiemann, S. U., Saretzki, G., Malek. N. P., Manns, M. P., Buer, J., Rudolph, K. L.,

Lee, M. M, Gomez, S L., Chang, J. S., Wey, M., Wang, R. T., Hsing, A. W. Soy and isoflavone consumption in relation to prostate cancer risk in China. *Cancer Epidemiol Biomarkers Prev.* 2003 Jul. 12(7): 665-8.

Lee I. P., Kim, Y. H., Kang, M. H., Roberts, C., Shim, J. S., Roh, J. K. Chemopreventive effect of green tea (camellia sinensis) against cigarette smoke-induced mutations (SCE) in humans. JCell Biochem Suppl. 1997. 27: 68-75.

Lee, John R., M.D. What your doctor will not tell you about menopause. New York. Warner Books, 1996.

Lee, John R., M.D. Hormone balance for men. Phoenix, AZ, 2003.

Li X. Y., Sarkar, F. H. Gene expression profiles of I3C- and DIM-treated PC3 human prostate cancer cells determined by cDNA microarray analysis. *Jnutr.* 2003 Apr. 133(4): 1011-9.

The Life Extension Foundation's Disease Prevention and Treatment. Expanded fourth ed. Hollywood, Florida: Life Extension Media, 2003.

Lobelenz, J. Extractum sabal fructus in the therapy of benign prostatic hyperplasia (BPH). *Tpk therapeutikon.* 1992. 6: 34-7.

Lobelenz, J. Extractum sabal fructus in the therapy of benign prostatic hyperplasia (BPH). *Tpk therapeutikon.* 1992. 6: 34-37.

Lowe, F. C., Ku, J.C. Phytotherapy in the treatment of benign prostatic hyperplasia: A critical review. *Urology.* 1996. 48: 12-20.

Lowe, F. C., Robertson, C., Roehrbom, C., Boyle, P. Meta Analysis of clinical trials of permixon. *J Uro.* 1999. 159(5) suppi: 257.

Lowe, F. C., Robertson, C., Roehrbom, C., Boyle, P. Meta analysis of clinical trials of Permixon. *J Uro.l* 1999. 159(5) suppi: 257.

Lu, R., Serrero, G. Resveratrol, a natural product derived from grape, exhibits estrogenic activity and inhibits the growth of human breast cancer cells. *JCell Physiol.* 1995 Jun. 179(3): 297-304.

Luzzi, G.A. Chronic prostatitis and chronic pelvic pain in men: aetiology, diagnosis, and management. *J Eur Acad Dermatol Venereol.* 2002 May. 16(3): 253-6.

Ma, Z., Hung Nguyen, T., Hoa Huynh, T., Tien, Do P., Huynh, H. Reduction of rat prostate weight by combined quercetin-finasteride treatment is associated with cell cycle deregulation. *J Endocrinol.* 2004 Jun. 181(3): 493-507.

Ma, Z. S., Huynh, T. H., Ng, C. P., Do, P.T., Nguyen, T. H., Huynh, H. Reduction of CWR22 prostate tumor xenograft growth by combined tamoxifen-quercetin treatment is associated with inhibition of angiogenesis and cellular proliferation. *Int J Oncol.* 2004 May. 24(5): 1297--304.

Mandressi, A., Tarallo, U., Maggioni, A., et al. Terapia medica dell'adenoma prostatico.

Manestar-Blazic T. Hypothesis on transmission of longevity based on telomere length and state of integrity. Med Hypotheses. 2004. 62(5): 770-2.

Marandola, P., Ravasi, S., Jallous, H., et al. Hypercritical COa extract of serenoa repens in vitro and in vivo increased efficacy. Presentation at the 1998 International Saw Palmetto Symposium of the American Herbal Products Assoc. Naples, Florida. 1998.

Marandola, P., Jallous, H., Bombardelli, E., et al. Main phytoderivative in the management of benign prostatic hyperplasia. *Fitoterapia.* 1997. 68(3): 195-203.

Mattel, F. M., Capone, M., Acconcia, A., et al. Serenoa repens extract in the medical treatment of benign prostatic hypertrophy. *TW Urol Nephrol.* 1990. 2(5): 346-50.

Messina, M. J. Emerging evidence on the role of soy in reducing prostate cancer risk. *Nutr Rev.* 2003 Apr. 61(4): 117--31.

Mettlin, C., Selenskas, S., Natarajan, N., Huben, R. Beta-carotene and animal fats and their relationship to prostate cancer risk. A ease-control study. *Cancer.* 1989 Aug. 1.64(3): 605--12.

Michaud, D. S., Augustsson, K., Rimm, E. B., Stampfer, M. J., Willet, W. C., Giovannucci, E. A prospective study on intake of animal products and risk of prostate cancer. *Cancer Causes Control.* 2001 Aug. 12(6): 557-67.

Milner, J., Allison, R., Elliott, J., et al. Opportunities and challenges for future nutrition research in cancer prevention: A panel discussion. *Nutr.* 2003. 133: 25028-25048.

Moore, M. Herbal tinctures in clinical practice. Southwest School of Botanical Medicine. Albuquerque, NM. 1996.

Morrissey, C., Watson, R. W. Phytoestrogens and prostate cancer. *Curr Drug Targets.* 2003 Apr. 4(3): 231-41.

Mortality: A cross-national study. *Journal of the National Cancer Institute.* 1998 Nov. 4. 90, (21): 1637-47.

Muller, N., Alteheld, B., Stehle, P. Tomato products and lycopene supplements: mandatory components in nutritional treatment of cancer patients? *Curr Opin Clin Nutr Metab Care..* 2003 Nov. 6(6): 657-60.

Murray, M. T. *The Healing Power of Herbs.* Rocklin, CA: Prima Pub, 1995:286-93.

Narayanan, B. A., Narayanan, N. K., Re, G. G., Nixon, D. W. Differential expression of genes induced by resveratrol in LNCaP cells: P53-mediated molecular targets. *Int J Cancer.* 2003 Mar. 20. 104(2): 204-12.

Narayanan, B.A., et al. p. 53/p. 21(WAF1/CIP1) expression and its possible role in G1 arrest and apoptosis in ellagic acid treated cancer cells. *Cancer Lett.* 1999. 136: 215--21.

Narayanan, B.A., et al. Interactive gene expression pattern in prostate cancer cells exposed to phenolic antioxidants. *Life Sci.* 2002. 70: 1821-39.

Narayanan, B.A., Re, G. G. IGF-II down regulation associated cell cycle arrest in colon cancer cells exposed to phenolic antioxidant ellagic acid. *Anticancer Res.* 2001. 21: 359-64.

Newell, C.A., Anderson, L., Phillipson, J. Herbal medicines: A guide for health-care professionals. London:The Pharmaceutical Press, 1996.

Neuhouser, M. L. Dietary flavonoids and cancer risk: evidence from human population studies. *Nutr Cancer.* 2004. 50(1): 1-7.

Norrish, A. E., Skeaff, C. M., Arribas, G. L., Sharpe, S. J., Jackson, R.T. Prostate cancer risk and consumption of fish oils: a dietary biomarker-based case-control study. *Br J Cancer.* 1999 Dec. 81(7): 1238-42.

Oesterling, Joseph, M.D., Moyad, Mark, M.P.H. The ABCs of Prostate Cancer. Madison Books, Lanham, Maryland, 1997.

Olson, D. F., Bames, R. L.. Serenoa repens (Bartr.) Small—saw palmetto (Drug plants, seed production). U.S. Dept. of Agriculture. Agric Handbook. U.S. Dept. Agric. 1974. 450: 769-70.

Om, A. S., Chung, K.W. Dietary zinc deficiency alters 5 alpha-reduction and aromatization of testosterone and androgen and estrogen receptors in rat liver. *J Nutr.* 1996 Apr. 126(4): 842-8.

Otto, U., Wagner, B., Becker, H., et al. Transplantation of human benign hyperplastic prostate tissue into nude mice: first results of systemic therapy. *Urol Int.* 1992. 48: 167--70.

Overmyer, M. Saw palmetto shown to shrink prostatic epithelium. *Urology Times.* 1999. 24(6): 1, 42.

Owen, D. R. Mood alteration with yoga and aerobic exercise may not be necessary. *Perceptual ills.* 1992. 75: 1333.

Paffenbarger, R. S. J., R.T. Hyde, A. L. Wing. Physical activity and incidence of cancer in diverse populations: A preliminary report. *American Journal of Clinical Nutrition,* 45, (Suppl.) (1987): 312.

Pathak, S. K., Sharma, R.A., Mellon, J. K. Cancer Biomarkers and Prevention Group, Department of Oncology, University of Leicester, LE2 7LX, UK. Chemoprevention of prostate cancer by diet-derived antioxidant agents and hormonal manipulation (Review). *Int J Oncol.* 2003 Jan. 22(1): 5-13.

Paubert-Braquet, M., Cousse, H., Raynaud, J. P., et al. Effect of the lipidosterolic extract of serenoa repens (Pennixon®) and its major components on basic fibroblast growth factor-induced proliferation of cultures of human prostate biopsies. *Eur Urol.* 1998. 33: 340-7.

Paubert-Braquet, M, Mencia Huerta, J., Cousse, H, et al. Effect of the lipidic lipidosterolic extract of serenoa repens (Permixon®) on the ionophore A23187-stimulated production of leukotriene B4 (LTB4) from human polymorphonuclear neutrophils. *Prostaglandins, Leukot Essent Fatty Acids.* 1997. 57(3): 299-304.

Paubert-Braquet, M., Richardson, F.O., Servent-Saez, N., et al. Effect of serenoa repens extract (Permixon®) on estradiol/testosterone-induced experimental prostate enlargement in the rat. *Pharmacol Res.* 1996. 34(3/4): 171-9.

Paul, William E. M.D. Fundamental immunology. fifth ed. Philadelphia: Lippincott- Raven, 2003.

Physical performance capacity and serum hormone concentrations during prolonged traning in elite weight lifters International Journal of Sports Medicine. 8, (1987, Suppl. 1)

Phillis, Bach. C. N. C. James F. Bach M.D. *Prescription for Nutritional Healing.* Third ed. New York: Avery, 2003.

Polednak, A. P. College athletics, body size, and cancer mortality. *Cancer.* 1976. 38: 38.

Ravenna, L., Di Silverio, F., Russo, M., et al. Effect of the lipidosterolic extract of serenoa repens (Pennixon®) on human prostatic cell lines. *Prostate.* 1996. 29: 219--30.

Ravindranath, M. H., Muthugounder, S., Presser, N., Viswanathan, S. Anticancer therapeutic potential of soy isoflavone, genistein. *Adv*

Exp Med Biol. 2004. 546: 121–65.

Redecker, K. D., Funk, P. Sabal extract WS 1473 in benign prostatic hyperplasia. *Extracta Urologica.* 1998. 21: 24–6.

Reece Smith, H. R., Memon, A., Smart, C. J., et al. The value of Permixon in benign prostatic hypertrophy. *Br J Urol.* 1986. 58: 36–40.

Reiling, B. A., Johnson, D. D. Effects of implant regimens (trenbolone acetate-Estradiol administered alone or in combination with zeranol) and vitamin D3 on fresh beef color and quality. *J Anim Sci.* 2003 Jan. 81(1): 135–42.

Resveratrol inhibits the expression and function of the Androgen receptor in LNCaP prostate cancer cells. *Cancer Res.* 1999 Dec. 1. 59(23): 5892–5.

Reynolds, J. E. F., editor. Martindale: The extra pharmacopoeia. 31st ed. London: The Pharmaceutical Press, 1996.

Rhodes, L., Primka, R., Berman, C., et al. (Merck Research Group). Comparison of finasteride (Proscar®), a 5 D reductase inhibitor, and various commercial plant extracts in *in vitro* and *in vivo* 5D reductase inhibition. *Prostate.* 1993. 22: 43–51.

Ripple, M. O., W. F. Henry, R. P. Rago, et al. Prooxidant-antioxidant shift induced by androgen treatment of human prostate carcinoma cells. *Journal of the National Cancer Institute.* 1997. 89: 40–48.

Rodler, I., Zajkas, G. Hungarian cancer mortality and food availability data in the last four decades of the 20th century. *Ann Nutr Metab.* 2002. 46(2): 49–56.

Rose, Marc R, MD. A Woman's Guide to Male Menopause. LA: Keats, 2000.

Rowland, D. L., Tai, W. Department of Psychology, Valparaiso University, Valparaiso, Indiana A review of plant-derived and herbal approaches to the treatment of sexual dysfunctions. *Sex Marital Ther.* 2003 May–Jun. 29(3): 185–205.

Saartok, T., Dahlberg, E., Gustafsson, J. A. Relative binding affinity of anabolic-andro-genic steroids: comparison of the binding to the androgen receptors in skeletal muscle and in prostate, as well as to sex hormone-binding globulin. *Endocrinology.* 1984 Jun. 114(6): 2100–6.

Sanderson JT, Hordijk J, Denison MS, Springsteel MF, Nantz MH, van den Berg M. Induction and inhibition of aromatase (CYP19) activity by natural and synthetic flavonoid compounds in H295R human adrenocortical carcinoma cells. Toxicol Sci. 2004 Nov;82(1):70-9

Sartor, L., Pezzato, E., Dona, M., Dell'Aica, I., Calabrese, F., Morini, M., Albini, A., Garbisa. S.,
Department of Experimental Biomedical Sciences, Medical School,

Padova, Italy. Prostate carcinoma and green tea: (-)epigallocatechin-3-gallate inhibits inflammation-triggered MMP-2 activation and invasion in murine TRAMP model. *Int J Cancer.* 2004 Dec. 10. 112(5): 823-9.

Saw palmetto. *The Lawrence Review of Natural Products.* 1994 Mar. 1-2.

Schneider, Y., Vincent F, Duranton B, et al. Anti-proliferative effect of resveratrol, a natural component of grapes and wine, on human colonic cancer cells. *Cancer Lett.* 2000 Sep 29.158(l): 85-91.

Severson, R. K.,A. M. Nomura, J. S. Grove, et al. A prospective analysis of physical activity and cancer. *American Journal of Epidemiology.* 1989. 130: 522.

Shahed AR, Shoskes DA. Oxidative stress in prostatic fluid of patients with chronic pelvic pain syndrome: correlation with gram positive bacterial growth and treatment response. *J Androl.* 2000 Sep-Oct. 21(5): 669-75.

Sharma S, Stutzman JD, Kelloff GJ, Steele VE. Screening of potential chemopreventive agents using biochemical markers ofcar-cinogenesis. *Cancer Res.* 1994 Nov. 15. 54(22): 5848-55.

Shenouda, N.S., Zhou, C., Browning, J.D., Ansell, P.J., Sakla, M.S., Lubahn, D.B., Macdonald, R.S. Phytoestrogens in common herbs regulate prostate cancer cell growth in vitro. *Nutr Cancer.* 2004.49(2): 200-8.

Shimada, H., Tyier, V. E., McLaughlin, J. L.. Biologically active acylglycerides from the berries of saw palmetto *(serenoa repens). J Nat Prod.* 1997. 60(4): 417-8.

Shippen, Eugene, M.D. & Fryer, William. *The Testosterone Syndrome.* New York: M Evans and Company, Inc., 1998.

Shoskes, D.A., Manickam, K. Herbal and complementary medicine in chronic prostatitis. *World J Urol.* 2003 Jun. 21(2): 109-13.

Shoskes, D.A., Hakim, L., Ghoniem, G., Jackson, C. L. Long-term results of multimodal therapy for chronic prostatitis/chronic pelvic pain syndrome. *J Urol.* 2003 Apr. 169(4): 1406-10.

Shoskes, D.A. Phytotherapy in chronic prostatitis. *Urology.* 2002 Dec. 60(6 Suppl): 35-7. Discussion p. 37.

Sies, H., Stahl, W. Lycopene: antioxidant and biological effects and its bioavailability in the human. *Proc Soc Exp Biol Med.* 1998 Jun. 218(2): 121-4.

Skowronski, R. J., Peehl, D. M., Feldman D. Vitamin D and prostate cancer: 1,25 dihy-droxyvitamin D3 receptors and actions in human prostate cancer cell lines. *Endocrinology.* 1993 May. 132(5): 1952-60.

Sokeland, J. Urological Clinic of Dortmund, Training Hospital of the

University of Munster, Germany. Combined sabal and urtica extract compared with finasteride in men with benign prostatic hyperplasia: analysis of prostate volume and therapeutic outcome. *BJU Int.* 2000 Sep. 86(4): 439-42.

Stellman, S. D., Takezaki, T., Wang, L., et al. Smoking and lung cancer risk in American and Japanese men: an international case-control study. *Cancer Epidermal Biomarkers Prev.* 2001 Nov. 10(11): 1193-9.

Stewart, J. R., Artime, M. C., O'Brian, C. A. Resveratrol: a candidate nutritional substance for prostate cancer prevention. *Nutr.* 2003 Jul. 133(7 Suppl): 2440S-2443S.

Strauch, G., Perles, P., Vergult, G. (Merck Research Group), et al. Comparison of finasteride (Proscar®) and Serenoa repens (Permixon®) in the inhibition of 5-alpha reductase in healthy male volunteers. *Eur Urol.* 1994. 26: 247-52.

Sultan, C., Terraza, A., Devillier, C., et al. Inhibition of androgen metabolism and binding by a liposterolic extract of serenoa repens B in human foreskin fibroblasts. *J Steroid Biochem.* 1984. 20(1): 515-9.

Takeoka, G. R., Dao, L., Flessa, S., Gillespie, D. M., Jewell, W.T., Huebner, B., Bertow, D., Ebeler, S. E. Processing effects on lycopene content and antioxidant activity of tomatoes. *J Agric Food Chem.* 2001 Aug. 49(8): 3713-7.

Tasca, A., Barullli, M., Cavazzana, A., et al. Treatment of obstructive symptomatology in prostatic adenoma with an extract ofserenoa repens. *Minerva Urologica e Nefrologica.* 1985. 37: 87-91.

Tchetgen, M. B., Song, J.T., Strawderman, M., Jacobsen, S. J., Oesterling, J. E. Michigan Prostate Institute, University of Michigan, Ann Arbor 48109, USA. Ejaculation increases the serum prostate-specific antigen concentration. Urology. 1996 Apr. 47(4): 511-6.

Terry, Paul, Paul Lichtenstein, Maria Feychting, Anders Ahlbom, Alicja Wolk. Fatty fish consumption and risk of prostate cancer. Lancet. 2001 June. 357(9270): 1764.

Thompson, L. Antioxidants and hormone-mediated health benefits of whole grains. Critical Reviews in Food Science and Nutrition. 1994. 5(6): 473-97.

Trabucco, A. Saw Palmetto Warning: Problems with Detecting Prostate Cancer. Presentation at the International Saw Palmetto Symposium, August 1998.

Tyagi, A., Agarwal, R., Agarwal, C. Grape seec extract inhibits EGF-induced and constitu-tively active mitogenic signaling but activates JNK in human prostate carcinoma DU145 cells: possible role in antiproliiera-tion and apoptosis. Oncogene. 2003 Mar. 6. 22(9): 1302-16.

Tyier,V. E.The honest herbal.Third ed. Binghamton, NY: Pharmaceutical Products Press, 1993: 285-7.

Udeani, G. O., Gerhauser, C.,Thomas, C. F., et al. Cancer chemopreventive activity mediated by deguelin, a naturally occurring rotenoid. *Cancer Res.* 1997 Aug. 15. 57(16): 3424--8.

Udo Erasmus. *Fats and Oils.*Burnaby BC:Alive Books, 1991.

Ulsperger, E., Hamilton, G., Raderer, M., et al. Resveratrol pretreatment desensitizes AHTO-7 human osteoblasts to growth stimulation in response to carcinoma cell super natants, *Int Joncol.* 1999 Nov. 15(5): 955-9.

Vahlensieck, W., Volp, A., Lubos, W., et al. Benign prostatic hyperplasia — treatment with Sabal fruit extract.A surveillance study on 1,334 patients. Fortschr Med. 1993. 111: 323-6.

Veierod, M. B., Laake, P.,Thelle, D. S. Dietary fat intake and risk of prostate cancer: a prospective study of 25,708 Norwegian men. Int Jcancer. 1997 Nov 27. 73(5): 634-8.

Vena, J. E., S. Graham, M. Zielezny, et al. Occupational exercise and risk of cancer.American Journal of Clinical Nutrition. 1987. 45: 318.

Vermeulen A, Kaufman JM, Goemaere S, van Pottelberg I. Medical Clinic, Section of Endocrinology, University Hospital, Gent, Belgium. Estradiol in elderly men.Aging Male. 2002 Jun;5(2):98-102.

Vincent T DeVita, Jr., Samuel Hellman, Steven A. Rosenberg. *Cancer principles and practice of oncology.* Sixth ed Philadelphia: Lippincott-Raven, 2004.

Wai, L. K.Telomeres, telomerase, and tumorigenesis—a review. *Med Gen Med.* 2004 July 26.6(3): 19.

Weisburger, J. H.American Health Foundation, One Dana Road,Valhalla, NY. Antimutagens, anticarcinogens, and effective worldwide cancer prevention. *J Environ Pathol Toxicol Oncol. 1999.* 18(2): 85-93.

Weisser, H., Behnke, B., Helpap, B., et al. Enzyme activities in tissue of human benign prostatic hyperplasia after three months' treatment with the Sabal serrulata extract IDS 89 (Strogen®) or placebo. *Eur Urol.* 1997. 31: 97-101.

Wilt, T. J., Ishani, A., Stark, G., et al. Saw palmetto extracts for treatment of benign prostatic hyperplasia. A systematic review. *JAMA.* 1998 Nov. 11. 280(18): 1604.

Wilt, T. J., Ishani, A., Rutks, I., MacDonald, R. Phytotherapy for benign prostatic hyperplasia. *Public Health Nutr.* 2000 Dec. 3(4A): 459-72.

Wolter, F., Turchanowa, L., Stein, J. Resveratrol-induced modification of polyamine metabolism is accompanied by induction ofc-Fos. *Carcinogenesis.* 2003 Mar. 24(3): 469–74.

Wynder, E. L., Taioli, E., Fujita, Y. Ecologic study of lung cancer risk factors in the U.S. and Japan, with special reference to smoking and diet. *Jpn J Cancer Res.* 1992 May.; 83(5): 418–23.

Xing, N., Chen, Y., Mitchell, S. H., Young, C. Y. Quercetin inhibits the expression and function of the androgen receptor in LNCaP prostate cancer cells. *Carcinogenesis.* 2001 Mar. 22(3): 409–14.

Yu, H., R. E. Harris, E. L. Wynder. Case-control study of prostate cancer and socio-economic factors. *Prostate.* 1988. 13: 317.

Yuan, H., Gong, A., Young, C. Y. Involvement of transcription factor Sp1 in quercetin-mediated inhibitory effect on the androgen receptor in human prostate cancer cells. *Carcinogenesis.* 2005 Jan. 20.

Yuan, H., Pan, Y., Young, C. Y. Overexpression of c-Jun induced by quercetin and resverol inhibits the expression and function of the androgen receptor in human prostate cancer cells. *Cancer Lett.* 2004 Sep. 30. 213(2): 155–63.

Zhao, J., Wang, J., Chen, Y., Agarwal, R. Anti-tumor-promoting activity of a polyphenolic fraction isolated from grape seeds in the mouse skin two-stage initiation-promotion protocol and identification ofpro-cyanidin B5-3'-gallate as the most effective antioxi-dant constituent. *Carcinogenesis.* 1999 Sep. 20(9): 1737–45.

Zhou, J. R., Yu, L., Zhong, Y., Blackburn, G. L. Soy phytochemicals and tea bioactive components synergistically inhibit androgen-sensitive human prostate tumors in mice. Nutrition/ Metabolism Laboratory, Department of Surgery, Beth Israel Deaconess Medical Center, Harvard Medical School, Boston, MA, USA. *J Nutr.* 2003 Feb. 133(2): 516–21.

Ziegler, H., Holscher, U., et al. Efficacy of saw palmetto fruit special extract WS 1473 in patients with stage I-II benign prostatic hyperplasia—open multicentre study. *Jatros Uro.* 1998. 14: 2–7.

Glosary

Abdominal- pelvic CT (computed tomography) scan: This is a procedure similar to an X-ray that images the organs in the abdomen and pelvis. Can be use to determine lymph nodes and other tissues affected by cancer.

Acid phosphatase: Also called prostate-acid phosphatase or PAP is an enzyme produced and released by the prostate gland, the liver, spleen and bone marrow. Abnormally high serum levels of the enzyme may, for example, indicate prostate disease (infection, injury, or cancer).

Acute Bacterial prostatitis: Inflammation of the prostate gland of sudden (acute) onset due to bacterial infection. The symptoms include chills, fever, pain in the lower back and genital area, body aches, burning or painful urination, and the frequent and urgent need to urinate. The urinary tract is infected, as evidenced by the presence of white blood cells and bacteria in the urine.

Adrenal gland: One of a pair of small glands, each of which sits on top of one of the kidneys. The adrenal is made up of an outer wall (the cortex) and an inner portion (the medulla). The adrenal glands produce hormones that help control the heart rate, blood pressure, the way the body uses food, and other vital functions. The adrenal cortex secretes steroid (cortisone-related) hormones and mineralocortoids that regulate the levels of minerals such as sodium and potassium in the blood. The adrenal medulla makes adrenaline (adrenaline) and noradrenaline (noradrenaline). Adrenaline is secreted in response to low blood levels of glucose as well as exercise and stress; it causes the breakdown of the storage product glycogen to the sugar glucose in the liver, facilitates the release of fatty acids from adipose (fat) tissue, causes dilation (widening) of the small arteries within muscle and increases the output of the heart. Noradrenaline is a neurohormone, a neurotransmitter, for of most

THE KEY TO HEALTHY PROSTATE AND ANDROPAUSE

of the so-called sympathetic nervous system.

Androgenic: Pertaining to the development of male characteristics, including body hair, the genital organs and muscle mass. "Androgenic" is the adjective form of the noun "androgen," a word referring to any of the male hormones, including testosterone and androsterone.

Androgens: These are male sex hormones. The most important is testosterone.

Andropause: Represent a change in male hormonal balance. Andropause is male menopause. As men age, testosterone levels go down, and conversion from testosterone to estrogen (estradiol) goes up. This is the definition in relation to hormones. By the time men are between the ages of forty and fifty-five, they can experience a phenomenon similar to the female menopause called andropause. Unlike women, men do not have a clear-cut signpost, such as the cessation of menstruation, to mark this transition.

Anesthesia: Loss of feeling or awareness. A general anesthetic puts the person to sleep. A local anesthetic causes loss of feeling in a part of the body such as a tooth or an area of skin without affecting consciousness. Regional anesthesia numbs a larger part of the body such as a leg or arm, also without affecting consciousness.

Angiogenesis: The process of developing new blood vessels. Angiogenesis is important in the normal development of the embryo and fetus. It also is important to tumor formation. For prostate cancer (or any other solid cancer) to survive, it needs a blood supply. There is an increasing research in substances (called antiangiogenesis substances) that not allow tumors to grow their own blood vessels.

Antibiotic: A drug used to treat infections caused by bacteria and other microorganisms. Originally, an antibiotic was a substance produced by one microorganism that selectively inhibits the growth of another. Synthetic antibiotics, usually chemically related to natural antibiotics, have since been produced that accomplish comparable tasks.

Aromatase enzyme: An enzyme involved in the production of estrogen that acts by catalyzing the conversion of testosterone (an androgen) to estradiol (an estrogen). Aromatase is located in estrogen-producing cells in the adrenal glands, ovaries, placenta, testicles, adipose (fat) tissue, and brain.

Arthritis: literally means joint inflammation; a general term for more than 100 conditions, known as rheumatic diseases, that affect not only the joints but also other parts of the body, including important supporting structures such as muscles, tendons, and ligaments, as well as some internal organs.

Benign: A term that means noncancerous.

Benign Prostatic Hyperplasia: Abbreviated BPH. A noncancerous prostate problem in which the normal elements of the prostate gland grow in size and number. Their sheer bulk may compress the urethra, which courses through the center of the prostate, impeding the flow of urine from the bladder through the urethra to the outside. This leads to urine retention and the need for frequent urination. If BPH is severe, complete blockage can occur.

Biopsy of the prostate: The sampling of tissue from different areas of the prostate, which is then examined to check for the presence of cancer.

Bladder: The organ in the pelvis that stores urine produced by the kidneys until urination occurs. One end of the bladder is connected to the ureter. Which carries urine from the kidneys; the other end is connected to the urethra, which carries urine out of the body through the penis.

Bone scan: A technique to create images of bones on a computer screen or on film. A small amount of radioactive material is injected and travels through the bloodstream. It collects in the bones, especially in abnormal areas of the bones, and is detected by special instrument called a scanner. The image of the bones is recorded on a special film for permanent viewing. Bone scans are used for the detection and monitoring of disorders affecting the bones, including Paget's disease, cancer, infections, and fractures. Bone scanning is also helpful in evaluating joint diseases.

BPH: See "benign prostatic hyperplasia."

Cancer: A general term for more than 100 diseases characterized by abnormal and uncontrolled growth of cells. The resulting mass, or tumor, can invade and destroy surrounding normal tissues. Cancer cells from the tumor can spread through the bloodstream or lymph system to start new cancers in other parts of the body.

Carcinoma: A malignant tumour arising from epithelial cells, which are cells lining the external or internal surfaces of the body. Carcinomas spread to nearby tissues. They may also spread to distant sites such as lung, liver, lymph nodes and bone.

Castration: Also called bilateral orchiectomy. Surgical removal of the sex glands usually used to indicate removal of the male testicles.

Catheter:A thin, flexible tube. For example, a catheter placed in a vein provides a pathway for giving drugs, nutrients, fluids, or blood products. Samples of blood can also be withdrawn through the catheter. It is usally refer toa tube that is inserted through the penis up the urethra and into the bladder. It is used to drain urine from the bladder.

CAT scan or CT scan:A computerized axial tomography scan is more commonly known by its abbreviated name, CAT scan or CT scan. It is an x-ray procedure which combines many x-ray images with the aid of a computer to generate cross-sectional views and, if needed, three-dimensional images of the internal organs and structures of the body. A CAT scan is used to define normal and abnormal structures in the body and/or assist in procedures by helping to accurately guide the placement of instruments or treatments.

Chronic bacterial prostatitis: Longstanding bacterial infection of the prostate gland superimposed on a defect in the prostate. (The prostate is a small organ below the bladder which surrounds the urethra, the tube that carries urine down from the bladder.) The symptoms can include low back pain, discomfort in the perineum (the area between the anus and the genitalia), testicular pain and, if the infection spreads to the bladder, mild pain or burning on urination (dysuria) and frequent and urgent need to urinate (frequency and urgency). The presence of white blood cells and bacteria in the urine attests to the fact that the urinary tract is infected with bacteria.

Clinical trials: Carefully controlled studies that are conducted in humans who volunteer to test the effectiveness and safety of new drugs, medical products or techniques. All drugs in the United States undergo three phases of clinical trials before being approved for general use.

Cognitive functions:The skills of the brain - memory, attention, and concentration.

Cryosurgery:Also called cryotherapy or cryoablation. Treatment performed with an instrument that freezes and destroys abnormal tissue.

DHT: See "Dihydrotestosterone."

Depression:An illness that involves the body, mood, and thoughts that affects the way a person eats and sleeps, the way one feels about oneself, and the way one thinks about things.

Digital rectal examination:An exam also called DRA; it is done to detect abnormalities that can be felt (palpated) from within the rectum. The doctor inserts a lubricated, gloved finger into the rectum and feels for anything that is not normal. The digital rectal exam is an important screening test for the detection of tumors of the rectum and prostate abnormalities, including benign enlargement of the prostate (benign prostatic hyperplasia) and cancer of the prostate.

DHEA: Dehydroepiandrosterone. A steroid hormone made by the adrenal glands that acts on the body much like testosterone and is converted into testosterone and estrogen. DHEA and its sulfate (DHEAS) are abundant in the body, but their normal roles are not fully understood. DHEA appears to facilitate improved cholesterol profiles, loss of body fat, increased muscle gain improve the immune system. The blood levels of DHEA and DHEAS decline with age.

Diabetes: A condition in which the body does not produce or respond to insulin (a hormone produced by your body, which allows blood sugar or glucose into your body's cells for energy).

Dihydrotestosterone: A byproduct of the male hormone testosterone. Dihydrotestosterone (DHT) is considered to be the essential androgenic hormone. DHT is responsible for the formation of male primary sex characteristics during embryonic life. It is responsible for the development of most secondary sex characteristics in males at puberty. And it continues to be important to male sexual function throughout adult life. It is also responsible for male baldness, prostate enlargement and prostate cancer.

Double- blind studies: scientific technique used to eliminate bias in a study, where neither the study participant nor the experimenter (doctor) knows which of two treatments the participant is receiving

DRE: See "digital- reactal examination."

Ejaculation: Ejection of sperm and seminal fluid.

Endurance: Endurance is the act of sustaining prolonged stressful effort.

Erectile dysfunction: A common men's health problem characterized by the consistent inability to sustain an erection sufficient for sexual intercourse or the inability to achieve ejaculation, or both. Impotence can vary. It can involve a total inability to achieve an erection or ejaculation, an inconsistent ability to do so, or a tendency to sustain only very brief erections. Erectile dysfunction is also called impotence.

Estradiol: The female hormone that is produced by cells that live in the follicle (nest) around the developing egg. There are three estrogens Estrone E-1, Estradiol E-2 and Estriol E-3. Males convert as they age testosterone into estradiol. In males estradiol can be responsible for prostate enlargement and prostate cancer.

Estrogens: Female hormones that also are made in males, especially as they age.

Fibromyalgia: A syndrome characterized by chronic pain, stiffness, and tenderness of muscles, tendons, and joints without detectable inflammation. Fibromyalgia does not cause body damage or deformity. However, undue fatigue plagues the large majority of patients with fibromyalgia and sleep disorders are common in fibromyalgia.

Five-alpha reductase: An enzyme in the prostate that can convert testosterone into a stronger form of testosterone called DHT or Dihydrotestosterone.

Follicle-stimulant hormone: Also called FSH. A hormone produced by the pituitary gland that controls estrogen production by the ovaries and simulates sperm production in the testicles.

FSH: See "follicle- stimulating hormone."

Gleason grading system: A grading system for prostate carcinoma devised by Dr. Donald Gleason in 1977 as a method for predicting the behavior of prostate cancer. On a total of 2 to 10, tumors with a low Gleason score are less likely to show aggressive behavior and therefore are less likely to have spread outside of the gland to lymph nodes (metastases). Gleason's original data showed a progressive increase in death due to the cancer with an increasing Gleason score.

Heart diseases: More than 2,500 Americans die each day from heart disease, the nation's number one killer! Many are struggling to recover from a heart attack, while others at high risk are getting the care they need and making the necessary changes to lower their risks

HIFU: See "high-intensity focused ultrasound."

High-intensity focused ultrasound: Also called HIFU is a treatment for benign prostatic enlargement; uses heat from ultrasound energy like a knife to trim excess prostate tissue that causes urinary problems.

Hormone: An active chemical substance formed in one part of the body and carried in the blood to other parts of the body where it stimulates or suppresses cell and tissue activity.

Hot flashes: A sudden wave of mild or intense body heat caused by rushes of hormonal changes. Hot flashes can occur at any time and may last from a few seconds to a half-hour. They are due to blood vessel opening and constricting.

Hyperplasia: The abnormal multiplication or increase in the number of normal cells in normal arrangement in a tissue.

Hyperthermia: Using the heat to treat benign prostate enlargement and prostatitis as well as other conditions, like hemorrhoids.

Immune system: A complex system that is responsible for distinguishing us from everything foreign to us, and for protecting us against infections and foreign substances. The immune system works to seek and kill invaders.

Impotence: A common problem among men characterized by the consistent inability to sustain an erection sufficient for sexual intercourse or the inability to achieve ejaculation, or both. Impotence can vary. It can involve a total inability to achieve an erection or ejaculation, an inconsistent ability to do so, or a tendency to sustain only very brief erections.

Incontinence: Inability to control excretions. Urinary incontinence is inability to keep urine in the bladder. Fecal incontinence is inability to retain feces in the rectum.

Inflammation: The body's response to tissue injury or infection which occurs in the affected tissues and adjacent blood vessels. The blood vessels' permeability is increased, and the area becomes heavily populated with white blood cells. Signs of inflammation are redness, swelling, pain, and sometimes loss of function. Not all of these signs are necessarily present in any given case.

Insulin: A natural hormone made by the pancreas that controls the level of the sugar glucose in the blood. Insulin permits cells to use glucose for energy. Cells cannot utilize glucose without insulin.

Invasive: Describes a procedure in which an incision is made or an instrument is inserted into the body through the skin or a body orifice, for diagnostic or therapeutic purposes.

Joint: A joint is the area where two bones are attached for the purpose of motion of body parts. A joint is usually formed of fibrous connective tissue and cartilage. An articulation or an arthrosis is the same as a joint.

Kidney: One of a pair of organs located in the right and left side of the abdomen which clear "poisons" from the blood, regulate acid concentration and maintain water balance in the body by excreting urine. The kidneys are part of the urinary tract. The urine then passes through connecting tubes called "ureters" into the bladder. The bladder stores the urine until it is released during urination.

Liver: large and complicated reddish-brown glandular organ located in the upper right portion of the abdominal cavity; secretes bile and functions in metabolism of protein and carbohydrate and fat; synthesizes substances involved in the clotting of the blood; synthesizes vitamin A; detoxifies poisonous substances and breaks down worn-out erythrocytes.

Lung: organ (pair) of the thorax whose contractions and expansions during respiration deliver oxygen to the blood

Luteinizing hormone (LH): A hormone released by the pituitary gland in response to luteinizing hormone- releasing hormone. Abbreviated LH, it controls the length and sequence of the female menstrual cycle, including ovulation, preparation the uterus for implantation of a fertilized egg, and ovarian production of both estrogen and progesterone. In males, it stimulates the testes to produce androgen.

Libido: Another word for sex drive, sexual desire, sexual drive.

Magnetic resonance imaging: MRI, a special radiology technique designed to image internal structures of the body using magnetism, radio waves, and a computer to produce the images of body structures. An MRI is painless and has the advantage of avoiding x-ray radiation exposure. There are no known risks of an MRI. The benefits of an MRI relate to its precise accuracy in detecting structural abnormalities of the body. An MRI may be used to see weather there is cancer in the prostate and if it has spread to other structures. Patients with heart pacemakers, metal implants, or metal chips or clips in or around the eyes cannot be scanned with MRI because of the effect of the magnet. Metallic chips, materials, surgical clips, or foreign material (artificial joints, metallic bone plates, or prosthetic devices, etc.) can significantly distort the images obtained by the MRI scanner.

Malignant: A term that mens cancerous.

Metastatis: The spread of cancer from one part of the body to another. Cells in the metastatic (secondary) tumor are like those in the original (primary) tumor.

MRI: See "magnetic resonance imaging."

National Cancer Institute: One of the National Institutes of Health (NIH) in the U.S., whose mission is to "lead a national effort to reduce the burden of cancer morbidity and mortality and ultimately to prevent the disease. Through basic and clinical biomedical research and training, NCI conducts and supports programs to understand the causes of cancer; prevent, detect, diagnose, treat, and control cancer; and disseminate information to the practitioner, patient, and public."

NIC: See "National Cancer Institute."

Osteoporosis: Thinning of the bones with reduction in bone mass due to depletion of calcium and bone protein. Osteoporosis predisposes a person to fractures, which are often slow to heal and heal poorly. It is more common in older adults, particularly post-menopausal women and also men; in patients on steroids; and in those who take steroidal drugs. Unchecked osteoporosis can lead to changes in posture, physical abnormality (particularly the form of hunched back known colloquially as "dowager's hump"), and decreased mobility.

Parkinson's disease: A slowly progressive neurologic disease characterized by a fixed inexpressive face, a tremor at rest, slowing of voluntary movements, a gait with short accelerating steps, peculiar posture and muscle weakness, caused by degeneration of an area of the brain called the basal ganglia, and by low production of the neurotransmitter dopamine. Most patients are over 50, but at least 10 percent are under 40.

PAP: See "Prostatic acid phosphatase."

Pathologist: A doctor who identifies diseases by studying cells and tissues under a microscope.

Perineum: The area between the scrotum and the anus

Pregnenolone: A precursor hormone made primarily in the adrenal glands, but also in the brain, liver, skin, and ovaries. It can convert to DHEA and progesterone and all the adrenal steroid hormones, including testosterone and estrogen.

Progesterone: a female sex hormone, produced by the ovaries during the second half of the menstrual cycle. In males can balance the effect of estradiol.

Prostate: A gland in the male reproductive system just below the bladder. The prostate surrounds part of the urethra, the canal that empties the bladder, and produces a fluid that forms part of semen

Prostate-specific antigen: also called PSA; a test for PSA may be used to screen for cancer of the prostate and to monitor treatment of the disease. PSA is a protein produced by the prostate gland. Although most PSA is carried out of the body in semen, a very small amount escapes into the blood stream. The PSA test is done on blood. Since the amount of PSA in blood is normally minute, the PSA test requires a very sensitive method based on monoclonal antibody technology. PSA in blood can be by itself as free PSA or it can join with other substances in the blood as bound PSA. Total PSA is the sum of free and bound forms. This is what is measured as the standard PSA test.

Prostatectomy: Surgical procedure that involes total or partial removal of the prostate.

Prostatitis: An inflammation of the prostate gland, usually due to infection.

PSA: See "Prostate-specific antigen."

Radiation therapy: Treatment with high-energy rays to kill or damage cancer cells. External radiation therapy is the use of a machine to aim high-energy rays at the cancer. Internal radiation therapy is the placement of radioactive material inside the body as close as possible to the cancer.

Radiotherapy: See "radiation therapy."

Rectal exam: See "digital examination."

Remission: Disappearance of the signs and symptoms of cancer or other disease. When this happens, the disease is said to be "in remission." A remission can be temporary or permanent.

Risk factor: Something that increases a person's chances of developing a disease.

Scrotum: A pouch of skin which contains the testes, epididymides, and lower portions of the spermatic cords.

Sebaceous glands: The glands of the skin that emit oil into the hair follicles.

Semen: The fluid that is released through the penis during orgasm. Semen is made up of fluid and of sperm. The fluid comes from the prostate, seminal vesicle and other sex glands. The sperm are manufactured in the testicles. The seminal fluid helps transport the sperm during orgasm. Seminal fluid contains sugar as an energy source for sperm.

Seminal vesicle: One of two glands located behind the male bladder, which secrete a fluid that forms part of semen.

SHBG: Also known as sex hormone binding globulin or proteins are present in the circulation and 90-99% of the steroid hormones in the circulation are associated with these proteins. The remaining 1-10% of the hormones are biologically active or "free". Changes in sex hormone binding globulin levels can significantly affect the ratio of free testosterone to estradiol levels in the plasma.

Staging: In regard to cancer, the process of doing examinations and tests to learn the extent of the cancer, especially whether it has metastasized (spread) from its original site to other parts of the body.

Symptomatic: An individual who is symptomatic is one who is experiencing symptoms of their disease.

Telomerase: An enzyme concerned with the formation, maintenance, and renovation of telomeres, the ends of chromosomes. Telomerase regulates the proliferative capacity of human cells. Telomerase activation plays a critical role in the progression of cancer as well as in normal somatic cells. Failure to activate sufficient telomerase promotes disease.

Telomere: The end of a chromosome, a specialized structure involved in the replication and stability of the chromosome.

Testicles: The testicles (also called testes or gonads) are the male sex glands. They are located behind the penis in a pouch of skin called the scrotum. The testicles produce and store sperm, and they are also the body's main source of male hormones (testosterone). These hormones control the development of the reproductive organs and other male characteristics, such as body and facial hair, low voice, and wide shoulders.

Testosterone: A "male hormone" — a sex hormone produced by the testes that encourages the development of male sexual characteristics, stimulates the activity of the male secondary sex characteristics, and prevents changes in them following castration.

Transrectal: Term refer to any procedure that is done throught the rectum.

Tumor: An abnormal mass of tissue that results from excessive cell division. Tumors perform no useful body function. They may be benign (not cancerous) or malignant (cancerous).

Urethra: The transport tube leading from the bladder to discharge urine outside the body. In males, the urethra travels through the penis, and carries semen as well as urine. In females, the urethra is shorter than in the male.

Urologist: A physician who specializes in diseases of the urinary organs in females and the urinary tract and sex organs in males. Also called a urological surgeon.

Watchful waiting: Closely monitoring a patient's condition but withholding therapy until the sign and symptom appear or change. Also called observation.

Index